England For All by H.M. Hyndman
First Prism Key Press Edition 2012

Prism Key Press
New York, NY 10001
PrismKeyPress.com

ISBN-13: 978-1475029291

England For All
H.M. Hyndman

CONTENTS

Preface

In this changeful period, when the minds of men are much troubled about the future, and many seem doubtful whither we are bound, I have attempted to suggest for the Democratic party in this country a clear and definite policy. The views expressed in this little work do not, I am aware, accord with the commonly received politics and economy of the day. Holding, as I do, strong opinions as to the capacity of the great English-speaking democracies to take the lead in the social reorganization of the future, I think it right to state them, and to show at the same time how seriously the working people suffer under our present landlord and capitalist system.

From the luxurious classes, as a whole, I expect little support. They have plenty of writers ready to champion their cause. To the people alone I appeal, and their approval will be my reward.

It was for the Democratic Federation that I originally wrote this book, and I present to its members the first copies to-day.

For the ideas and much of the matter contained in Chapters II and III, I am indebted to the work of a great thinker and original writer, which will, I trust, shortly be made accessible to the majority of my countrymen. [1]

June 8th 1881
10 Devonshire Street
Portland Place
LONDON W

Notes

1. A reference to Karl Marx. The lack of acknowledgement by name apparently gave offence. – *ERC*

Introduction

It is impossible to survey our modern society without at once seeing that there is something seriously amiss in the conditions of our every-day life. All may indeed lament the inequalities around them, the wasted wealth and excessive luxury of the rich, the infinite misery and degradation of the poor. So clear is the mischief which results from causes apparently beyond control, that now and then a paroxysm of self-reproach seizes upon the comfortable classes, and they try some new-fangled scheme of charity to remedy the ills which, for the moment, they think must be due to them. But this temporary feeling is very short-lived. The conditions of human existence are said to be unchangeable by collective, far less by individual, action, and religion is often called in to justify the let-alone policy which is so far the most convenient to the well-to-do.

Possibly, however, a change is at hand. In England as elsewhere, ideas in these days move fast. That disgust with both the political parties in the State which has long been felt by the more intelligent of the working-class – that rooted impression that men in broadcloth, no matter how they label themselves, are banded together, in spite of their pledges at the polls, to keep the men in fustian from their fair share of the enjoyments of life, is spreading now from the abler men to the less far-sighted. More and more clear is it becoming to our people that their interest in politics is something which, if fully understood, lies far deeper than that of their daily or weekly wage. "We working men," said one, "shall never know our real interest in politics till the mother teaches the truth about them to her child;" and this phrase by itself happily shows that a very different view of the duty of the community to all is growing up from that indifference and sluggishness which have hitherto checked progress. How could it be otherwise? Is it conceivable that the men who make the wealth of the country will permanently be satisfied with a system which shuts them out for ever from all interest in their own land? that they will be content to live from hand to mouth on the strength of mere phrases, and that they will always consent to be deprived of their due share of representation? They are indeed shortsighted who so suppose. Now therefore it becomes necessary that people of all classes who desire that our existing society should be peacefully modified should be content to examine, a little more deeply than heretofore, into the present state of things.

This, so far as the wealthy are concerned, from the most selfish point of view; for there is nothing here in the eternal fitness of things. The evolution of mankind will not stand still, in order that landowners and capitalists may continue their present leisurely existence, or that the well-to-do generally may regard the sufferings of the toilers as of small account. Such poverty as now exists is not an inseparable accompaniment of human society; neither is such excessive concentration of wealth an incentive to human progress. The gospel of greed and selfishness, of corruption and competition, now proclaimed as the only means of social salvation, is seen to be false in its principles, and baneful in its results. This furious development of wealth, on which we sometimes congratulate ourselves, has done little to elevate, and much to lower, the tone even of the classes which have benefited by it. What has it done for the working class? Never at any period in our history were the many who work and the few who live upon their labour so wide apart, socially and politically, as they are to-day; never – and this is becoming in itself serious – has there been such a general sensation of uneasiness without any immediate cause.

Yet who can wonder that uneasiness there should be? Political reforms have done very little for our people. Periods of flash prosperity, speedily followed by depression which pinches and starves even the best artisan class; education progressing so slowly that still another generation will be suffered to grow up instructed enough only to be ignorant; overcrowded insanitary dwellings permitted to continue, and paid for at an exorbitant price because this is to the benefit of the classes who trade upon the necessities of their fellows; vast monopolies encouraged and overwork checked, – here we have the boasted freedom of the latter half of the nineteenth century. The very champions of free trade as the universal panacea are themselves driven to confess that, true though their theory is, it has not produced the social effect they predicted. [1] The rich have grown richer; but the poor – their condition is but little bettered, and relatively has gone back. Our civilization is in many respects but an organized hypocrisy, filming over as ulcerous places below as ever disgraced the worst periods of past history. But there is something more than hypocrisy or indifference to account for the crying evils of our great cities, and the miserable poverty and bad lodgment which degrades our agricultural population. More general causes than any which individuals can right, are at work. Private enterprise has been tried and found wanting: laissez-faire has had its day. Slowly the nation is learning that the old hack arguments of "supply and demand," "freedom of contract," "infringement of individual liberty," are but so many bulwarks of vested interests, which inflict misery on the present, and deterioration on the next, generation, in the name of a pseudo-science of government. Bad as is the education of the majority of Englishmen compared with what it ought to be, they have learnt enough to be dissatisfied with arrangements which, when more ignorant, they might have accepted as inevitable. Of the sufferings which the real producers of this great industrial community undergo, the comfortable classes hear but little. They barely talk of their troubles to their most intimate friends. The natural inclination of Englishmen is to bear in silence. Hitherto many have found consolation in religion, which held out to them the prospect of happiness hereafter in return for sorrow and misery here. That resource is now failing, and the bolder spirits – it is useless to blink plain truths – openly deride those "drafts on eternity" which they say are issued solely in the interest of employers and rich men. Their own ills nevertheless they may bear: that they will consent to hand on the same lot to their children is very unlikely. The day for private charity and galling patronage is at an end; the time for combination and political action in redress of social wrongs is at hand.

Such changes as are needed may be gradual, but they must be rapid. In England, fortunately, we have a long political history to lead up to our natural development, the growth of a great nation such as ours has its effect on all portions of the people. Patriotism is part of our heritage; self-restraint necessarily comes from the exercise of political power. Even the poorest are ready to accept the assurance of real reform, rather than listen to those who would urge them to resort in desperation to violent change. Yet these reforms must in the end be far more thorough than the enthusiasts of compromise, and the fanatics of moderation are ready to admit. Hitherto there has been patience, because all have hoped for the best. But longer delay is not only harmful but dangerous. We are ready enough to talk about justice to others. Greeks, Slavs, Bulgars, Boers, Negroes, are ever appealing to our sense of what is due to the oppressed. Let the people of these islands, without despising others, now be just to themselves. If the theories now gaining ground all over the Continent, as well as here with us, are to be met peacefully, and turned to the advantage of all, the necessary change of front can no longer be delayed. The State, as the organized common-sense of public opinion, must step in, regardless of greed or prejudice, to regulate that nominal individual freedom which simply strengthens the domination of the few. Thus only shall the England of whose past we all are proud, and of whose future all are confident, clear herself from that shortsighted system which now stunts the physical and intellectual growth of the great majority, knit together the great

12

democracies near and far under our flag, and deal out to our dependencies a full measure of that justice which alone can secure for us and for ours the leadership in the social reorganization which will be our greatest claim to respect and remembrance from countless generations of the human race.

Notes

1. Two professors of the straitest sect of economic orthodoxy, Mr. Henry Fawcett and Mr. Thorold Rogers, are of the same opinion on this point. Free trade is undeniably true in theory, but they agree that it has benefited the poor very little in comparison with the enormous wealth it has given to the rich. Free "trade lowers the price of the necessaries of life; but it also keeps wages lower than they otherwise would he. It would be easy to show that the working classes owe all the improvement that has been made in their condition, not to free trade, but to combination among themselves, and to legislation carried directly in the teeth of the most violent opposition from the leaders of the free trade party.

Chapter I The Land

Possession of the land is a matter of such supreme importance to the liberty and well-being of Englishmen, that the only marvel is not that there should be a growing agitation on the subject to-day, but that the nation should ever have been content to bear patiently the monopoly which has been created during the past 300 years. It affords indeed a strange commentary upon the history of human progress, that we have to look back more than 400 years to the period when the mass of the people of these islands were in their most prosperous and wholesome condition. In those middle ages which our school-books still speak of as days of darkness and ignorance, the great body of Englishmen were far better off in every way than they are now. The men who fought in the French wars, and held their own against every Continental army, were sober, hard-working yeomen and life-holders, who were ready to pay for their victories out of their own pockets, instead of saddling their descendants with a perpetual mortgage in the shape of a huge national debt. They owned the soil and lived out of it, and having secured for themselves power at home and freedom by their own firesides, they kept them.

The fifteenth century was the golden age of agricultural England. Villenage had disappeared; the country – far more populous at that time than is commonly supposed – was occupied and cultivated by free men, who tilled their own lands, subject only to light dues payable to feudal superiors. Such day-labourers as there were, lived in perfect freedom, owned plots of land themselves, and shared in the enormous common land which then lay free and open to all. Landless, houseless families were almost unknown, permanent pauperism was undreamt of. The feudal lords who maintained around them crowds of retainers were at this time merely the heads of a free, prosperous society, which recognized them as their natural leaders alike in war and peace. Notwithstanding, or rather by reason of the great subdivision of land, the wealth of the bulk of the people was extraordinary. They were their own masters, and could speak their own minds freely to all; the degrading servility of the agricultural labourer of today had not appeared to take the place of the thraldom of the old serfs. No description ever given of any people shows a more prosperous set of men than the Englishmen of that time. Their sturdy freedom was based upon property and good living.

"The King of England cannot alter the laws or make new ones without the express consent of the whole kingdom in Parliament assembled. Every inhabitant is at his liberty fully to use and enjoy whatever his farm produceth, the fruits of the earth, the increase of his flock, and the like; all the improvement he makes, whether by his own proper industry or of those he retains in his service, are his own to use and to enjoy without the let, interruption, or denial of any. If he be in any wise injured or oppressed, he shall have amends and satisfactions against the party offending. Hence it is that the inhabitants are rich in gold, silver, and in all the necessaries and conveniences of life. They drink no water, unless at certain times, and by the way of doing penance. They are fed in great abundance with all sorts of flesh and fish, of which they have plenty everywhere; they are clothed throughout in good woollens; their bedding and other furniture in their houses are of wool, and that in great store. They are also provided with all other sorts of household goods, and necessary implements for husbandry. Every one according to his rank hath all things which conduce to make life easy and happy."

This was merrie England, in short – merrie, that is, for Englishmen as a whole, not merely for the landlords and capitalists at the top, who live in ease on the fruits of their labour. For a day-labourer, a plain, unskilled hand – with his

16

geese, and sheep, and cow on the common – could then get something for his day's work. That of course is the real test of the comfort and well-being of the mass of the people, at all periods and under all governments – what food and what clothing a man can get for so many days' work.

A common day-labourer, then, in the fifteenth century could earn a fat sheep by four days' work, a fat ox by twenty days' work, and a fat hog two years old by twelve days' work. Clothing he could obtain on at least equally good terms. His own labour for others and on his own plot supplied him and his family well with all "the necessaries and conveniences of life." Those even of the poorer sort lived upon beef, pork, veal, and mutton every day. There is no dispute about this. There are the recorded lists of prices for food, drink, and raiment, the rates paid in parish after parish for unskilled labour. Men so different as Cobbett and Fawcett, Thornton and Rogers, are all agreed on these points. They are of one mind, that the working agriculturist of the fifteenth century was a well-to-do free man.

How do our present agricultural labourers figure in comparison? How much of such fare as that given above are hired labourers on ten and twelve shillings a week likely to get, and what sort of houses do they too often inhabit? We all can judge of that, even if the reports of Agricultural Commissions were not at hand to tell us. The agricultural labourer of to-day is a mere pauper beside his ancestor of 400 years ago, who probably owned the land out of which the landowner and the farmer now permit his descendant to work a scanty subsistence which barely enables him to taste meat once a month. His wages are shameful and his cottage a disgrace. What is the reason then of all this increasing penury, accompanied in rural districts by an astounding decrease of population? Unquestionably the entire removal of the people from the land is the chief cause of the mischief. Those yeomen and free farmers, and fat well-fed labourers, who secured for us those liberties which of late years have been made such surprisingly little use of were turned out, and the history of how it was done, and how our present hand-to-mouth population was formed, is not a pleasant tale. The mass of men have now no real freedom either in country or town, because the land has been taken by the great landholders and never yet restored to the nation at large. Thus the sense of property, of ownership, individual or collective, is done away.

From our own land still comes the bulk of the wealth of the country, the food, the ores, the coal, which enable us to hold our own, and get a return from other parts of the world. But the workers who do this for England have no part nor lot in their country of today. They own nothing but their bare right to compete with their fellows in the labour-market. Who can fail in such circumstances to recall these stirring words?

"Freedom is not an empty sound; it is not an abstract idea; it is not a thing that nobody can feel. It means, and it means nothing else, the full and quiet enjoyment of your own property. If you have not this – if this be not well secured to you, you may call yourself what you will, but you are a slave. Now our forefathers took special care upon this cardinal point. They suffered neither kings nor parliaments to touch their property without cause clearly shown. They did not read newspapers, they did not talk about debates, they had no taste for 'mental enjoyments;' but they thought hunger and thirst great evils, and they never suffered anybody to put them on cold potatoes and water. They looked upon bare bones and rags as indubitable marks of slavery; and they never failed to resist any attempt to affix these marks upon them."

And we too hold much the same opinions, and we too regard pauperism and destitution as disgraces to a free country. But unfortunately this generation, and others before it, have grown up to think such "indubitable marks of slavery" unavoidable, and hold too that land should rightfully belong in perpetuity to the handful of men who drove the mass of the population from the soil, or who bought from the descendants of those who did. But the life of a nation like ours outlasts all such temporary troubles; its rights, though long in abeyance, are never done away. The truth that the land of England belongs to the people of England is coming home to men of all classes; and the best proof that our existing system will no longer be borne with contentment is that the historical wrong which has been done is daily more and more considered.

That revolution which supplied England with a bountiful succession of paupers, and laid the foundation of landlordism in the country, and of capitalism in the towns commenced in the last quarter of the fifteenth century and the beginning of the sixteenth. After the wars of the Roses had impoverished the nobility, the dismissal of numerous baronial households launched upon the country a whole horde of landless people, without house or home. These unfortunates had no place whatever in society as it then existed, and became at once mere vagrants and competitors for all sorts of chance employments. But for the monasteries and other religious establishments their condition would have been far worse than it was. Even these outcasts, however, might have been gradually absorbed; but about the same time the great nobles, who were at variance with the crown and the parliament, set to work to restore their fortunes by turning out the peasant owners, who under the feudal law had at least as good a title as their own to their holdings. Such raids were followed up by encroachments on the common lands, which the labourers depended upon for depasturing their animals. Accompanying these robberies also was a steady conversion of arable land into pasture, on the ground that more was to be gained by feeding sheep than men – a contention which has of late been put forward also in Scotland, Ireland, and in newly-settled countries. To compete profitably in the wool-markets of Flanders was more important than to maintain a race of independent peasant farmers.

19

These changes worked a deplorable deterioration in the condition of the mass of the people. The number of the agricultural population who could find employment in the old way rapidly lessened. Even now, with our improved methods of cultivation, and labour saving machinery, arable land will employ more than twice as many men as pasture – and raise more beasts, for that matter, as well. But in those days the proportion was probably far larger. At any rate, numbers were thrown out of employment in that way. So serious did all this become that Henry VII and his Parliament made constant efforts to check the vicious and harmful action of the barons; but unfortunately to little purpose. The people were more and more interfered with, and depopulating enclosures were going on regularly. Laws were even framed of the most stringent character to prevent ejection of the peasants and the destruction of their houses. All without effect. The landless class still increased, and more and more people became dependent on others for support. Henry VII., a great though penurious monarch, saw clearly that the welfare of the mass of his subjects, not the inordinate wealth and aggrandizement of the few, constituted the real strength of his kingdom, however much he might attempt to fleece them by monopolies out of part of their substance. He was anxious therefore to keep the land in the hands of the small owners, who were really the bone and sinew of the country. Even the day-labourer received consideration, and was secured by the laws four acres of land to his cottage. But the process of expropriation went relentlessly on notwithstanding, and had already produced a serious effect.

But the confiscation of the lands of the monasteries, and priories, and nunneries, at the time of the Reformation, was a far graver blow to the welfare of the people. Carried out with a shameless disregard for the rights and privileges of the people, by the most violent and despotic monarch who ever sat on the English throne, this was the greatest injury inflicted on the poor which our history records. The property of the Catholic Church, though not always well administered, was in reality at the service of the poor and needy. Whatever might be urged against abbots and friars, pauperism was then unknown. The celibate parish priests had small expenses, and the land they held was held, it may almost be said, in trust for the people. The yeomen and labourers on their estates, never disturbed or interfered with from generation to generation, were a prosperous, vigorous folk. Besides, the service of the Church was almost the only career, except successful murder, by which a poor lad might in those days rise to the highest dignities of the State. Prelates and monks were founders of our noblest schools of learning. They were, however, swept away, their goods seized, and the lands taken from the people, to be held by the king or given to his favourites. Parliament then, as later, was bribed to sanction illegal and improper action, by which many of its members largely profited. King and barons were once more knit together in that happy participation in plunder which has been the surest bond of union between monarchs and aristocrats all over the world. Thus the poor who had ever obtained ready relief from the Church, the wayfarers who could always find food and shelter in the religious houses, the children of the people who repaired to the convent for guidance and teaching, were deprived at one fell swoop of alms, shelter, and schools.

When, however, the monasteries were thus destroyed, and their lands confiscated for the benefit of the King and the aristocracy, not only was almost the last hold of the English people on their own soil torn off, but the monks and nuns, priests and friars, were turned loose upon the world to swell the ranks of the have-nots. The shiftless hand-to-mouth class thus grew with fearful rapidity. The whole country was overrun with loafers and vagrants, deprived of the means of living by no fault of their own. Not even the most atrocious laws could keep them within limits, though they drove them into the towns, and into the power of the shopkeeping class, now gaining strength. Paupers being thus numerous, in the 43rd year of Elizabeth –

who had resumed all the confiscated lands – a Poor Law was passed; and from that time to this pauperism has formed as integral a portion of our social constitution as the aristocracy who created the necessity for the law. How could it be otherwise? The landed rights of the many had been sacrificed to the greed of the few; and confiscation, really put in force to bolster up luxury and selfishness, was carried on in the name of religion.

Between the fifteenth and the beginning of the seventeenth century the whole face of England had been changed. In place of well-being, contentment, and general prosperity, as described by Fortescue, depression and misery had become the common lot of the people who owned no land. The mere wage-earner took the place of the labouring, petty farmer – a man at the mercy of his employer. For the fine old yeoman class fell more and more into decrepitude, and the downfall of the ecclesiastical property preceded their own final ruin by but a short interval. Yet even so late as the end of the seventeenth century eighty per cent. of the population of England was still purely agricultural. By the middle of the eighteenth century there was scarcely a yeoman of the old type left in a county.

The Stuarts were bad enough, but William III was worse than any of his immediate predecessors. This great Whig hero treated England as if he had conquered it in respect to all he could lay hands upon, and gave away lands he had no right whatever to dispose of to his thick-headed and greedy Dutch followers. Their descendants prey upon us to this hour, though, with the exception of Lord William Bentinck, not a single one of them has been of the slightest genuine service to the State whose land they have seized, or has illustrated our history even by mischance in the field. All this long series of robberies from the people, helped on by economical causes, ended in an aggregation of property and influence in a few hands to an extent never before equalled.

It was followed by an enclosure of the common kinds of a character even more nefarious. Parliament, made up almost exclusively of landowners, and in no sense whatever representative of the mass of the people, framed bill after bill for the enclosure of the commons, which alone were left to show that the soil of England had formerly been looked upon as the property of the great majority. No man, not a landlord, can read through the records of this disgraceful pillage even now without a feeling of furious bitterness. Nothing more shameful is told in the long tale of class greed than this of the seizure of the common lands by the upper and middle classes of Great Britain. To deprive the people of their last vestige of independent holding, and thus to force all to become mere hand-to-mouth wage-earners at the mercy of the growing capitalist class, such was the practical effect of these private enactments, conceived in iniquity, and executed in injustice. For up to so recent a date as 1854 these enclosures were done by private bill, and of course exclusively in private interest. There was no public discussion whatever; and rich men who coveted a few thousand acres of common which belonged to their poorer neighbours, simply laid hands upon them and added them to their estate. Fierce protests were often made in the neighbourhood, but they were invariably unavailing. In the course of 150 years, between 1700 and 1845, no fewer than 7,000,000 acres of public land, and probably a great deal more, were enclosed by the landowners of England in Parliament assembled, without one halfpenny of real compensation ever having been made to the public whose rights were thus ridden over. At that time, be it remarked, the people of England – but shabbily represented now – had practically no voice in public affairs at all, and such a man as Sir Robert Walpole just "ran the machine" in the sole interest of his class, for all the world like a Pennsylvanian log-roller or wire-puller of our own day. Not even scraps of those great and valuable common lands remain in some districts to remind the English people of the robberies that have been committed upon them.

Even since the introduction of public bills to regulate these enclosures matters were, until quite lately, very little better. A wealthy landgrabber would purchase land all round a common, and then stealthily get it enclosed on some shallow pretext. This occurred over and over again. The hard fight which such a body as the Corporation of the City of London had to wage in order to keep for the people of London what remnant there is of Epping Forest, shows the pertinacity with which individual selfishness works on. Conservatives and Liberals who stand up for the ancient and indefeasible rights of property at the expense of others should look into these things. The very people who ate up the whole country away from their countrymen and make land a monopoly, cry out fiercely that they are being ill-used and robbed when an attempt is made to reassert some small portion of the rights of the nation over that which is, and always has been, the property of the nation – the land of England. What sort of title have many of them to their lands? Let them answer who made the laws which gave the eternal right to harm the people. Why, they themselves and their fathers before them. None other. The owners of the land had no voice; violence, wrong, and fraud, weigh still upon the country. But there need be no fear for those who profited by these encroachments. The people are never unjust, even in their own interest: they pay to get back their simplest rights.

The effect of this seizure of the commons upon the rural population has been most sad. Their condition, never very flourishing since they were deprived of individual ownership, became yet worse. But I will quote a calm writer, who is fully convinced of the beneficial effects of supply and demand, and freedom of contract: – "Many of the descendants of those who once possessed valuable rights of common are agricultural labourers, to whose miserable condition allusion has already

24

been made. Our rural population has been deprived of that which once gave a most important addition to their income. The common often enabled them to keep some poultry, a pig, and a cow. Many villages may now be traversed, and not a single labourer can be found possessing a head of poultry; few even keep a pig, and not one in 10,000 has a cow. What is the result of this? The labourer does not live as he did 100 years since; he and his family seldom taste meat, and his children suffer cruelly from the difficulty he has in obtaining milk for them." This, indeed is a matter of common consent. The agricultural labourer is far worse off than his forefathers. But if the people have been deprived of their commons, so also have their plots of ground to their ill-drained, overcrowded cottages disappeared. They make them too "independent." No property, low diet, a pretence of education, and enforced servility to their "betters" – that was the way to bring down the "proud peasantry" from their high looks of the fifteenth century to the abasement of a ten-shilling-a-week agricultural labourer, ever begging for some dole out of the fruits of his own labour to be given back to him, from the Hall, the Rectory, or the poorhouse, This kept him "in that state of life" which the Church Catechism enjoins upon the lowly. No agricultural labourer, it needs hardly be said, has ever yet sat in the House of Commons to represent the wrongs of his class.

These unfortunate families, deprived of their own land and ousted from their common lands, became, as we have seen, fair game for the most abominable legislation. The laws against vagrants and men out of work were ferocious and brutal, to a degree scarcely to be credited until they were actually revived in America the other day. By these means they came into the towns, where, refused the right to combine, and wholly destitute of means, they were delivered over to a form of tyranny the more trying from its being carried on under the name of freedom. The very idea that the unfortunate had a definite interest in the country was done away. The poor were only not criminal. And this feeling grew among the dominant class with the growth of that shopkeeper spirit which has been paramount with English parties, to the almost entire exclusion of any sense of justice to the bulk of the community. The few landowners of genuine old family who still remain, and who, one would have thought, would look back with pride to the times when their ancestors were the leaders of well-to-do free men, have been as bad as the rest. They have thought that their duties, such as they were, began and ended with their tenantry. If the labourers received a fair amount in charity after having worked their lives through on starvation wages, that was as much as they could expect. The eternal law of supply and demand justified meat once a fortnight, and short commons all the year round. There stood the workhouse: what more *could* the people want?

But now what has been the outcome to us of to-day of all these uncompensated expropriations in England – of the ducal *razzias* like those of the Dukes of Sutherland and Argyll in Scotland (the latter worthy peer now naturally standing out with his fellow Liberal of Lansdowne in favour of the perpetuation of serfdom in Ireland) – what do we of the present generation derive from all this long succession of past iniquities? Nothing is easier than to sum it all up. We have then a great body of landowners, 2,000 of whom alone hold actually 8,000,000 acres of our land in estates of over 5,000 acres each, the total agricultural rental of this vast domain being not less than £25,000,000 annually. The whole of the agricultural land in the kingdom is practically owned by less than 30,000 persons; and not all the systematic fudging resorted to in the Landlord's Return, known as the "New Doomsday Book," has been able to shake that fact out of the minds of the people of England. In that book Lord Overstone formerly Mr. Jones, a banker of enormous wealth, who turned landgrabber after the manner of his kind – the Duke of Buccleuch, and the Duke of Devonshire are put forward as thirty-three different owners. This is only a specimen of how the truth is blinked and covered up by those who are interested in hiding it away from their countrymen. And this

26

monstrous monopoly the landowners, and the big capitalists who hope to be landowners, and their friends and relations the lawyers, who live upon the complications of the laws they themselves have formulated, are now striving to perpetuate.

Not to speak of the injurious consequences politically of such a concentration of excessive wealth and power in a few hands, the economical drawbacks stare us in the face. Men who own half-a-dozen large properties in several different counties must be permanent absentees from some of them. They take the rents and spend them elsewhere, being themselves the heaviest of all the burdens on the land. The majority of landowners cannot do justice to the land they have taken even in their own narrowest sense. Cumbered up with mortgages, settlements, rent-charges, heaven knows what, they are in no case to face a great fall in rents, to encounter competition from without, or to bring to bear that skill, labour and personal attention now essential to success in agriculture. The sacred trinity of landlord, capitalist-farmer, and agricultural labourer has broken up. The labourer can be screwed no lower, the farmer has had enough of giving his capital to the landlord as rent. American "wheat centres" have proved clearly that landlords are not an essential element in English agricultural production. A great change is therefore at hand. Agricultural experts aver with confidence that if the land of England were properly handled, if sufficient labour and manure were applied, we could profitably produce twice the quantity of food we do from the existing cultivated acreage. What stops us? Unquestionably that determination of landowners to hold on to their false idea of greatness, and to those miserable customs of settlement and entail which will necessarily be put an end to as a wider and more useful method of dealing with our soil opens up before us. Happily the landlords are themselves beginning to feel the pinch, and may lead the way in the reforms which have now become essential. If they do not it is no great matter; for sooner or later the people of England mean to have back the land, and the sooner the better for the interest of the landlords themselves.

For let it be remembered that the dominant classes have done more than take the land; by their Parliaments they have actually shuffled on to the shoulders of the mass of the people nearly all the taxes and obligations which formerly came out of their rents as a portion for the State and the poor. Laws enacted by men for their own benefit in direct contravention of the tenure on which the lands were originally taken have no binding force whatsoever on posterity. Yet the landowners of Great Britain were formerly subject to a land-tax of four shillings in the pound on their assessment. This they have whittled away almost to nothing, and now the land-tax under their skilful manipulation, produces but £1,074,919, instead of £18,802,337 as it ought. That is to say, the landowners of Great Britain put into their pockets a sum of little less than£18,000,000, which, but for their own self-gratifying ordinances would, according to the old laws of this kingdom, have gone into the treasury of the country at large. No wonder that our privileged classes and their hangers-on howl "confiscation," "communism," "socialism," and words more English and less nice, when any fearless man begins to rake up the history of their "sacrifices" to patriotism.

True patriots they; for be in unsderstand

They robb'd their country for their country's good!

But this is not all either. Agricultural property is well enough in its way, but the mines, all that underlies the soil has fallen also into the grip of the small minority, and it is impossible to get a bill through Parliament which will even compel the owners to protect the lives of the men who work in them. The miners should know their place, and have power to "contract out of the Act." What matters the risk of loss of life? Then the urban properties, again, with their vast unearned increment of rent, and the power given to individuals to obstruct improvements whilst they benefit by the expenditure of the public money or railroads carried through by the decision of Parliament. What, in the name of all that is reasonable, have Grosvenors or Bentincks for instance done for England that they and theirs should interfere for ever with the management of London, and pocket increasing rents which, if exacted at all, should go to the municipality which must shortly be created for this great metropolis, and benefit the whole community? Is it well that millions should be spent on the Thames embankment, for instance, and that landowners should pocket thousands a year by the improvement of their property? These are points which come home to all, and must, ere long, force on a change. Such enormous revenues as those which were squandered in digging catacombs in Welbeck Park, or laid out in providing Westminster with a dukedom, ought not to be at the unrestrained disposal of any single family. For no idea whatever of duty is attached to these great possessions; and artisans' dwellings, or a market, in a fashionable locality might "damage the property," and so are warned off.

How is it that the landowners themselves, or such at least as come fairly by their property, do not see that their political future depends upon recognizing the vast changes going on beneath them, and endeavour to associate themselves with the future of their country? Their object, one would think, would be necessarily to meet and guide that flow of democratic opinion which manifestly precedes a new social evolution. To stand on the brink and wring their hands in dismay is both cowardly and foolish. For in a small, densely-peopled country like ours the whole hangs together – land in country and land in towns, mines, communications, all go to make up the complicated system under which we live.

But agricultural land of necessity stands first. Mr. Clare Read says that all will come right, and that twenty-five years or so hence the territorial grandee will rise again to the enjoyment of his unearned increment, the farmer shall be a man of wealth and substance, and the agricultural labourer – well, what tenant-farmer ever thinks much about him? Landlord-made laws must undergo revision in the interests of the landlords themselves, but far more for the sake of the mass of their countrymen now dissociated altogether from the land. It is humiliating to look back fifty years, and note how little has been done since the able band of democratic writers, headed by Cobbett, first forcibly pointed out the historical injuries from which Englishmen are still suffering. As it was yesterday, so it is to-day; but so shall it not be to-morrow. The importance of the Land Question in England is now fully understood by the inhabitants of the counties as well as of the towns, and up to a certain point a vast majority will combine to overthrow the existing system, which lies like a dead weight upon it.

When we come to the direction in which changes should be made, however, the widest differences arise. Some seem to imagine that mere free trade in land, even without the plan of compulsory subdivision, would bring about the planting of the people on the land; others look upon the removal of settlement and entail as only preliminary to nationalisation, in the sense that by limitation of the right of inheritance and compulsory purchase at a valuation, the State, the county, or the municipality should come into the possession of all land within a calculable period. All depends upon what we desire to bring about. Many ardent reformers look forward to the day when English farmers shall hold their ten, twenty, fifty-acre farms, interspersed with larger holdings, as in former times. Is this to be done? Can we thus put back the clock 400 years? It would scarcely seem so; and yet on the whole it should appear that small farmers who depend chiefly on their own labour for their return have suffered less in all parts of the country, and have been readier to pay rent, than the large. In America also, the unincumbered farmer holding no large extent of land fared on

30

the whole better than his wealthier neighbour, who was growing not for produce so much as for profit.

The main object necessarily is to get as much out of the land as possible, and at the same time to secure the agricultural labourer, and those of the townspeople who take to the land, a fair return for their labour, and a prospect of obtaining possession of land if they desire to do so. Evidently the labourer and the townsman will gain nothing by giving the farmers in England fixity of tenure, nor much by free-trade in land. All evidence goes to show, however, that even under present conditions the more secure the tenure, in an increasing ratio up to freehold, the better on the whole the farming, until the limit of acreage is reached where the owner thinks he can afford to lie by and make an income by letting to others. But the present tenants would be no better employers as owners, or tenants on a permanent settlement, than they are now; the agricultural labourer who really does the work would still get his ten and twelve shillings a week, his cottage would be equally destitute of garden. On the other hand, if the capitalists came in, does their behaviour in the large cities make us very hopeful of what would take place under their management in the country? These are difficulties which at once arise in any scheme of individual improvement. Even the virtual limitation of the amount of land which may be held by any individual by means of cumulative taxation – the only fair taxation by the way – might not give the labourer on the land that independence which would enable him to hold his own. What the better, in short, would the mass of the population be for any of the reforms proposed? Granting that twofold would be produced, would the labourers or the urban population get a greater share of it? No doubt the diminution of the absurd social influence attaching to the ownership of land would have a great effect in lowering its value to a mere idler, especially if the game laws are speedily repealed. But all this does not help the man who does the work for ten and twelve shillings a week to get some fair portion of the fruits of his labour – to secure a decent home, a plot of ground, least of all a small farm. What is being done for Ireland, then, ought on a larger scale to be done here; though unfortunately want of education and knowledge cripples the present generation, and they have been more completely uprooted from the soil than even the Irish.

We are manifestly here, as elsewhere, in a transition period. The stage of dominant landlordism is passing away rapidly—that of State management, or co-operation in the interest of all, has apparently not nearly been reached. Granting therefore that the completest reforms of the land laws, in the shape of abolition of settlement and entail, complete subdivision, simplified registration, mortgage made illegal, and so forth, have been carried, much will remain to be done. Private enterprise cannot satisfactorily deal with the many important changes to be made. Benevolent investments at five per cent. are, in American parlance, "a fraud." What a miserable hand-to-mouth creature the agricultural labourer is to-day we know. Let, then, that point be borne in mind in all reforms, that until the labourer is placed in a position where he is really able to contract freely, either by combination, or by State assistance in the shape of permanent leases of land, subject to disturbance only for bad culture or non-payment of fair rent, no great change will ever be made in his condition for the better. For this too is for the interest of all. The titles of the landlords are none so good that they can afford any longer to run the risk of the cry, "The land for the people." Hitherto powers of expropriation and interference have been used solely in the interest of the upper and middle classes, who hold the control. Ere long a similar process may be demanded by the great majority in their favour, though not with equal injustice.

As stepping-stones to further development, the following reforms may be demanded at once:–

• Reform of the law of settlement and entail,

putting an end to the existing system altogether.

- Compulsory registration of title, so as to make transfer of land as easy as it is in America.
- Extension of the powers of local bodies to acquire land for all purposes and to lease it in small portions.
- Compensated expropriation of property-owners in large cities.

No confiscation or revenge for the forced removal of the people from the land is asked for. But the unborn have no rights, and the nation has always both the power and the right to take any land at a fair valuation. By immediate limitation of the right of inheritance, and an application of the power of purchase, the State or the local authority would speedily come into possession of land, which could be used for the common interest, and some comfort and security obtained for those who at present have neither. No longer then should the agriculturist be permanently kept away from the soil; no longer should the dweller in the city feel that, happen what might, he could never leave the street or alley. Hitherto the State has been regarded as an enemy: the time is coming when perhaps all will be ready to recognize that its friendly influence is needed to prevent serious trouble, and to lead the way to a happier period. That the landowners of England should join in a resolute endeavour to remedy the mischiefs which affect them in common with the rest of the population is apparently too much to expect. True, their interest lies in this direction. To stir up class hatred is easy enough, when, in spite of all sentimental talk and useless charity, the men who work see that nothing is really done which will permanently benefit them. A higher ideal than mere selfishness may indeed be held up, but those who are rich and powerful must lead the way. Of this truer patriotism there is at present no sign among those who claim to be the "natural leaders" of the people.

Chapter II Labour

In every civilized society the main point to be considered is the manner in which labour is applied to production, and the share of his own labour which in one shape or another the labourer gets in return. The ancient historical civilizations were chiefly built upon slavery. Here the labourer, his force of labour, and the material on which he expended it, all belonged to the master; and the wealth of the latter might almost be gauged by the number of slaves he possessed, though only a portion of them would be actually employed in the work of production. This employment of slave-labour renders any comparison between the state of society then and now almost futile; but the condition of the poor freemen in Rome and Athens, constantly exposed to the competition of slave-labour if they desired to work themselves, resembled that of the mean whites in the Southern States before the Civil War. The peasant proprietor, or the member of a village community, holds again a totally different position from that of the slave or the labourer of modern times. The peasant proprietor, or the craftsman owning his own tools and able to obtain his own materials, is master of himself, of his means of production, and of his produce, even though he may have to pay a portion of the latter to a feudal chief or rajah. In both cases, that of individual proprietorship and that of ownership in common of the produce of a community, there may be and generally is perfect freedom, save the restrictions which arise from the necessity of producing sufficient for the social necessaries of life.

It is quite possible that a man and his family may live on the produce of their own farm, carry on the simple operations of manufacture necessary to clothe them, and rarely have the need to exchange anything which they possess for the work of others. A good harvest, or a favourable season with cattle, will represent so much extra wealth, which will provide against bad times, or enable the little household to devote more labour to increase of comfort. With a village community the necessity for exchange may arise less often; for these units of civilization comprise within themselves the means of providing all the ordinary needs, and some even of the luxuries of life. It is to the interest of the whole family or village community that all should be well nourished and strong for the daily duty; it is also advisable that a certain provision be made against the prospect of bad seasons. Civilization, therefore, presupposes great forethought its earlier stages, or it would soon fall back again to the condition of the Paraguayans, who ate the seed given them by the missionaries. But all the wealth thus produced by the work of individuals or communities is clearly due to labour; and that is not wealth which is not recognized as an object of utility tin social conditions of the time.

The great majority of economists before and since Adam Smith have agreed that labour is the source of value. "The real price of everything," says Adam Smith himself, "what everything really costs to the man who wants to acquire it, is the toil and trouble of acquiring it. What everything is really worth to the man who has acquired it, and who wants to dispose of it or exchange it for something else, is the toil and trouble which it can save to himself, and which it can impose on other people. Labour was the first price – the original purchase-money that was paid for all things. In that early and rude state of society which precedes both the accumulation of stock and the appropriation of land, the proportion between the quantities of labour necessary for different objects seems to be the only circumstance which can afford any rule for exchanging them for one another. If among a nation of hunters, for example, it usually costs twice the labour to kill a beaver which it does to kill a deer, one beaver would naturally be worth, or exchange for, two deer. It is natural that what is usually the produce of two days' or two hours' labour should be worth double of what

36

is usually the produce of one day's or one hour's labour."

"That this," adds Ricardo, "is really the foundation of the exchangeable value of all things, excepting those which cannot be increased by human industry, is a doctrine of the utmost importance in political economy. If the quantity of labour realized in commodities regulate their exchangeable value, every increase of the quantity of labour must augment the value of that commodity on which it is exercised, as every diminution must lower it." This labour, of course, includes the work necessary to replace the wear and tear of tools and machinery, as well as the labour which is actually expended on and realized in the commodities. Every useful article produced by labour has two values, its value in use alone, and its value in exchange. Its value in use is developed only by being used and consumed: its value in exchange consists in obtaining other useful articles in its place.

Water, air, virgin soil, &c., are useful, but by themselves they constitute no value. A man may also expend his labour on useful articles which never become commodities or goods for exchange. These may be destined simply for his own use, and never for exchange. In all countries, however, where the capitalist system of production prevails, wealth appears in the shape of an accumulation of commodities or merchandise. Those products of human labour devoted to natural objects are exchanged according to the average quantity of human labour expended in producing them. If wheat and axes are exchanged in definite proportions, they are thus bartered with reference to the common element in each, by virtue of which an equality between them is established. This is the quantity of human labour expended in bringing them forward for exchange. So many days of average labour embodied in one article of utility, are equal to so many days of average labour embodied in another article of utility. Thus then the general rule is, that labour is the basis of value, and quantity of labour the measure of value of commodities, or social values for the use of others, all the world over. [1]

Say that a coat is worth twice as much as ten yards of cloth. The coat is useful and satisfies a particular want. Two kinds or qualities of labour are embodied in it – that of the tailor who made the coat, and that of the weaver who wove the cloth. So far as its usefulness is concerned also, it makes no difference whether the tailor wears it or his customer. Now as to its value. The coat is assumed to be worth twice as much as the ten yards of cloth – worth that is, twenty yards of cloth. In point of value coat and cloth as well are but expressions of labour itself. Thus the coat is worth twice as much as the cloth, because the cloth contains only half as much human labour; and it needs twice the quantity of labour to produce the coat complete, cloth and all, as to produce the cloth alone. Reduce the quantity of labour needed to make a coat by one half, and two coats are only worth what one was before. Double the quantity of labour needed to make a coat, and one coat is worth what two were before. In the same way, "if a piece of cloth be now of the value of two pieces of linen, and if, in ten years hence, the ordinary value of a piece of cloth should be four pieces of linen, we may safely conclude that either more labour is required to make the cloth, or less to make the linen, or that both causes have operated." Thus then, no matter whether the productive power of average human labour in producing any article of utility – and utility is, of course, an essential element of exchangeable value – is increased or diminished, the same length of labour, or the same quantity of labour, always represents the same value. But of course, if the labour is more productive, more values in use are obtained in given time, and if less productive, less: only the value for exchange remains unaltered.

But the above illustrations are easily extended. When a coat is said to be worth twice as much as ten yards of cloth, or worth that of twenty yards of cloth, this means, as has been said, that the quantity of human labour contained in the one is equal to, or expressed in, the quantity of human labour contained in the other. So with other articles of utility. A coat may likewise be equal in value to ten pounds of tea, or to half a ton of iron, or to a quarter of wheat, or to two ounces of gold; all these products of human labour being also equal in value to twenty yards of cloth, and varying in exchangeable value in proportion to the amount of labour embodied in them; the simple meaning of the equality being that the tea, the iron, the wheat, the gold, and the cloth, represent, each and all, the same quality of labour in the several amounts of commodities.

But it so happens that it has been found convenient for ages to express this general form of value in one particular commodity. This in nowise changes the fundamental proposition that labour is the basis of value, and quantity of labour its measure. The only further result is, that the coat, the ten pounds of tea, the half a ton of iron, the quarter of wheat, the twenty yards of cloth, are all equal in value, not only to one another, but to the two ounces of gold, which henceforward are taken as a measure of value for them all and become money. When commodities now are valued, they are valued with reference to the gold, which forms not only a real but an ideal valuation. It is not the money which enables the commodities to be valued. Far otherwise. It is because all commodities represent realized human labour already expended on natural objects, thus producing articles of utility, that their relative value is consequently measureable by one another, and that they can all be valued together in one special commodity. This last becomes money, and is a measure for them all, though, like the rest, its value consists in the fact that it represents the expenditure of human labour.

But money is not only a convenient measure of value, but also a means of putting commodities in circulation. A commodity is exchanged for its equivalent in money, and then again the money is exchanged for another commodity. In order to promote a circulation of commodities there must be a sufficiency of money, or the representative of money in some form of currency, to avoid congestion. To bring about the regular interchange of articles of utility in civilized life, such a change of commodities for money, and again into commodities, being the rule. This fact formed the basis of the theory of the celebrated Law, who desired to substitute for gold and silver, which cost labour to produce, and yet are in themselves of little utility, paper certificates of labour expended, which would cost nothing, and yet serve the purposes of currency. Without however, entering upon the phenomena connected with money, it is now clear that in all exchangeable value the human labour expended is the basis of the value of commodities, and the quantity of human labour the measure.

There is, of course, nothing new in all this. That natural objects are of no value unless human labour is expended on them is a truth as old as the world. That labour is the real basis, not only of value but of all civilized society, needs no elaborate demonstration at this time of day. Yet it is precisely from this generally admitted but little regarded truth that consequences follow of the highest importance to our modern society. Here come in those "differences of value," those strange manipulations of the worth of commodities, which go to the root of all business.

A merchant has a sum of money, say a hundred pounds sterling. Therewith he buys on the market suppose a hundred pounds' worth of cotton. So far the exchange may be perfectly fair and exact. The merchant has given his labour as expressed in a hundred pounds sterling for another man's labour as embodied in a mass of cotton. But, having bought, he goes away and sells his purchased cotton to another person for £110, making, as it is said, £10 by the transaction. His £100 was turned into its equivalent in merchandise, and then appeared again as £110. Not only is the original sum replaced, but more is added, and the merchant's money becomes capital. The merchant buys not for himself, or to work up for the use of others, but merely to sell the cotton again at an enhanced price. This is something very different from the use of money as the measure of the value of commodities, or as the means of facilitating exchange. It is commercial capital, which its owner takes upon the market for the purpose of increasing it. Money to start with; and then, after a longer or a shorter interval, more money – that, leaving out the intermediate process of buying the cotton, is the process. But the amount of value in circulation at any given moment – that is, the quantity of human labour on the average embodied in commodities – cannot increase of itself. If a merchant has in his possession a commodity whose value is expressed in money by £10, this value can only be increased absolutely, and made say £11, by the addition of more labour to the labour-value represented in the first instance as by making a coat of cloth. The coat is worth more than the cloth, but the value of the cloth remains the same. Thus then all conditions remaining the same, the owner of the money to start with must buy a piece of merchandise at its exact value, and sell it again for what it is worth, and yet have at the end more value than he had at the beginning.

Now the problem begins to take shape.

The increase of value by which money becomes more money and is turned into capital, obviously cannot arise from the money itself. It follows then that the conversion of money into merchandise, and then of that same merchandise into more money, is due to the merchandise. But how? Commodities can no more increase their own exchangeable value than money. In order to obtain an additional exchangeable value from a commodity, a sort of merchandise must be found which possesses the remarkable quality of being itself the source of exchangeable value, so that to consume it would be to obtain

41

that labour-force embodied in value, and consequently to create value.

Now it so happens that the capitalist in embryo does find on the market a purchaseable commodity endowed with this specific virtue. This is called labour, or force of labour. Under that name is comprised the entire capacities, physical and intellectual, which exist in the body of a man, and which he must set in motion in order to produce articles of utility. Evidently the force of labour cannot present itself on the market for sale, unless it is offered by its owner; he must be able to dispose of it – that is, be the free owner of his labour, of the force of his own body. The moneyed man and he meet on the market; one buys, and the other sells, and both are quits. But the owner of this labour-force must only sell it for a definite time; if he sells it for an indefinite time, from being a merchant, he himself, his force of labour and all, becomes a mere commodity. He is a slave or serf at the command of his master as a chattel. The more essential condition for the capitalist to be able to buy the force of labour is, that the owner of the labour instead of being able to keep himself by work on his own land, or to sell goods on which he has himself expended his labour, should be obliged to sell the labour-force in his body pure and simple. A man in order to sell goods of his own making, must of course command the means of production – tools, raw material, &c. Then he is master of his own labour, an independent man; he has the means of exchanging his own labour as embodied in useful articles, for other men's labour also embodied in useful articles, upon equal terms. But in order that money should be converted into capital, the workman himself must be free in a very different sense; not only must he be ready to sell his labour as a commodity, but further, he must be *free* – so very free that he has nothing else in the world but his power of labour to sell – that he should be completely destitute of the means of realizing his own force of labour in commodities by himself, having neither tools, nor land, nor raw materials wherewith to do so.

How does this free labourer thus find himself on the market, ready to enter into free contract? That does not concern the owner of the money, who looks upon the labour-market as a mere branch of the rest of the market for commodities, and governed by the same laws. The appearance of this destitute labourer there is nevertheless, as has been seen, the outcome of a long series of economical evolutions and revolutions extending over centuries. Driven from the land, deprived of the possibility of earning a living, the mass of the people find themselves concentrated in the towns. Nature most assuredly does not turn out possessors of money or goods on the one side, and owners of their pure labour-force, and nothing else, on the other; nor is such a social state common to most periods of history. So long, for example, as the produce of labour is used to supply the needs of the labourer, it does not, as has been seen, become merchandise; in the same way, the production and circulation of commodities may take place under many forms of society. It is not so with capital; that only makes its appearance when that part of the wealth of a country which is employed in production, consisting of food, clothing, tools, raw materials, machinery, &c., necessary to give effect to labour, is found in the hands of an owner, who meets on the market the free labourer come thither to sell his labour.

Capital then forms an epoch in social production.

What, however, is this force of labour, which the free owner of it comes on to the market to sell? Clearly it is a human force, physical, moral, intellectual, which requires certain material, food, and clothing and lodging – all in the possession of the moneyed man, and not of the labourer – to keep it in order and supplied, so that the waste of one day may be made good, and it may return with equal vigour the next. These necessaries vary, of course, with different climates, and with different degrees of civilization; but in any given country and period the average needs of the labourers are known. Nor is this fact altered by the other face that, as pointed out by Mill, a series of circumstances may reduce the standard of supposed necessaries. The amount of average necessaries thus ascertained is called by Ricardo, the "natural price of labour," and is "that price which is necessary to enable the labourers one with another to subsist, and to perpetuate their race without either increase or diminution." In this way we have that amount of average daily necessaries which will maintain the present race of destitute bargainers, and provide them with equally destitute successors.

Assume then that the cost of this amount of daily foods, the natural price of human labour comprised in the necessaries for existence for the twenty-four hours – representing by rights only the quantity of human labour expended in their production – is six hours' work. Half a day's average work is needed then to reproduce the average amount of labour-force expended. Take this at three shillings as expressed in money. Then the owner of the labour who sells its work for six hours at three shillings, sells it for its exact value. "It is when the market price of labour exceeds its natural price that the condition of the labourer is flourishing and happy that he has it in his power to command a greater proportion of the necessaries and enjoyments of life. When the market price of labour is below its natural price, the condition of the labourers is most wretched; then poverty deprives them of comforts which custom renders absolute necessaries." So far Ricardo again. But the natural price of labour reaches its minimum when it is reduced to the value of the means of subsistence physiologically indispensable. When it falls to this minimum, the price has reached a level below the value of the labour-force, which then only just maintains itself without immediate deterioration. For example, a man who sells his labour for just enough to keep himself and his family without making any provision for old age, or future ill-health from which he may suffer, is clearly going down hill. The natural price of his labour has not in this case taken a sufficiently wide range.

When also the capitalist buys the labour, it is the owner of that labour who sells on credit. He advances his labour to the capitalist; the capitalist advances nothing to him without having been previously paid for it. In every country where the system prevails, the labourer is only paid after he has worked for a certain period – a week, a fortnight, a month – on credit. This enables the capitalist to "turn round." If the employer fails, the labourers suffer: they are not paid; for the labour has been sold beforehand, and duly delivered by the expenditure of force from the labourer's body. An illustration of this occurred not long since in the great strike of colliers in the north against the masters, who wished to make their men break the law by contracting out of the Employers' Liability Act. Once out on strike they insisted most strongly upon the reduction of the length of the advance of their labour to the capitalist, from the fortnight to the week. This point also they carried. Fortnightly or monthly wages are a hardship to the labourer, which, like many others, can only be removed by resolute combination; for that value in use which the owner of the labour advances to the buyer, only shows itself in employment. And this consumption of force of labour produces, not only commodities, but surplus value besides. Everything else needed for the purposes of production – raw materials, machinery, &c. – have been bought by the capitalist at their actual value, and paid for at their actual price. It is labour only, the labour-force of human beings, from which he derives his surplus value. Out of this, his last purchase, bought on credit, the capitalist makes his capital breed. This labour, bought in the open market, and realized in the commodity – this it is which gives the capitalist the additional value he hungers for.

Now we begin to see how it comes about that £10. turns into £11, that £100 swells into £110, without additional value. Now, too, the admirable working of "freedom of contract" and "supply and demand" in our modern society appears. Hear, too, William Cobbett for a moment: "To those who labour, we who labour not with our hands owe all that we eat and drink and wear, all that shades us by day and that shelters us by night, all the means of enjoying health and pleasure; and therefore if we possess talent for the task, we are ungrateful or cowardly, or both, if we omit any effort within our power to prevent them from being slaves. What is a slave? For let us not be amused by a name. A slave is in the first place a man who has no property; and property means something that he has, and that nobody can take from him without his leave or consent. A slave has *no property in his labour*; and any man who is compelled to give up the fruit of his labour to another at the arbitrary will of that other, has no property in his labour, and is therefore a slave, whether the fruit of his labour be taken from him directly or indirectly. If it be said that he gives up the fruit of his labour by his own will, and that it is not forced from him, I answer, To be sure he *may* avoid eating and drinking, and may go naked; but then he must die; and on this condition, and this condition only, can he refuse to give up the fruit of his labour. 'Die, wretch, or surrender as much of your income or the fruit of your labour as your masters choose to take'."

To return. The working man who has sold his labour works, of course, under the control of the capitalist to whom his labour thus belongs, and whose object it is that he should work hard and continuously. Besides, the product in which his force of labour is embodied is the property of the capitalist, and in no sense that of the labourer. The capitalist merely pays him his wages, just as he would pay for the hire of a horse or a mule. Then the employer applies the human merchandise he has thus bought to his raw materials and machinery. The result is a value in use to be passed on to others; and not only such value, but a surplus value for the capitalist himself, derived from this purchased labour.

Take, for example, cotton yarns. The capitalist buys, say, ten pounds of raw cotton for 10s. In that price there is already expressed the average labour needed for the production, transport, and marketing of the raw cotton. Now put the wear and tear of the spindles, machinery, &c., in working up the raw material into yarn at 2s. If a piece of gold of the value of 12s. is the output of twenty-four hours' work, it follows that there are, apart from the labour in the factory, two full days of work embodied in the yarn. This accounts for the original labour needed to raise and transport the raw cotton, as well as the labour needed to replace the wear and tear.

It has already been assumed that the workman must give six hours' labour in order to earn 3s., the natural price of his labour required to supply him socially with his absolute necessaries. Now assume further that it takes six hours' labour to turn ten pounds of cotton into ten pounds of yarn; then the workman has added to the raw cotton a value of 3s., a half-a-day's work. So at the end the ten pounds of yarn contain altogether two days and a half of labour; raw cotton and wear and tear of spindles stand for two days; and half-a-day has been absorbed by the cotton in the process of spinning. This quantity of labour is therefore reckoned in a piece of gold of the value of 15s.; that is to say, the price of the yarn worked up from the cotton is 1s. 6d. a pound. Here obviously is no gain to the capitalist. His raw material, his wear and tear of machinery, his wages paid for the labour which he has purchased, eat up the whole of the capital advanced, and yet the ten pounds of yarn only fetch 1s. 6d. a pound, which is the value of the average quantity of labour contained in it. This shows no profit whatever, much to the horror of the capitalist if he stopped there.

But the employer has bought the labourer's whole day's work upon the market. He can make him work therefore not merely the six hours required to produce the return of the 3s.

paid, but twelve hours – a day's work. Now if six hours' work produces ten pounds of yarn from ten pounds of cotton, twelve hours' work: will give twenty pounds of yarn from twenty pounds of cotton. These twenty pounds of yarn will thus contain five days' labour, of which four are contained in the raw cotton and the wear and tear of machinery and spindles, and one day is absorbed by the yarn during the process of spinning. The expression in money then of these five days' work is 30s. That, therefore, is the price of the twenty pounds of yarn. Thus the yarn is sold now as it was before at 1s. 6d. a pound. But the sum of the values of the merchandise (including labour in the factory) embodied in the yarn does not exceed 27s.; that is to say, 20s. for the raw cotton, 4s. for the wear and tear, and 3s. for the labour in the factory. The value of the product has therefore increased. The 27s. have become 30s. Those 27s. advanced by the capitalist have begotten a surplus value of 30s., and the trick is done. The capitalist has used a certain amount of another man's labour for his own behoof without paying for it, and the trick is done at that man's expense. That free labour which is sold in the open market enables the capitalist to sell the twenty pounds of yarn he has made at the regular price of 1s. 6d. a pound, and, nevertheless, to increase his capital by 3s. on the output of twenty pounds. Labour thus used is the origin of surplus value, and all's well.

Once more it is permissible to look back to the £10 made into £11 to the £100 swollen into £110. The £1 like the £10 is obtained from that free labour which is bound to be sold for less than its worth, in order that its possessor may continue to keep body and soul together. And the surplus value so produced the capitalist, the merchant, the shopkeeper, divide among themselves.

In existing conditions of agricultural production, the agricultural labourer in the same way provides on his part the surplus value which the landowner, the rent-charger, the farmer, the mortgagee, divide, in the shape of rent, settlement, profit on capital, and interest on money lent. The labourer himself, earning his 10s. to 12s. a week, is the man upon whom all these worthy people live, though they do so in a more indirect manner than the capitalist of the large towns, and have perhaps a trifle more conscience left to appeal to.

Capital itself, however, is divided into two parts, that which is used to buy machinery and means of production, and that which is expended on labour. The former portion is constant, and is simply reproduced without increase, the latter is variable, and is that which produces surplus value. Ordinarily the rate of surplus value is calculated on the total amount of capital employed, constant and variable, and is dubbed profit on capital. But this is wholly incorrect. The rate of surplus value produced, the proportion of labour turned to account by the capitalist should be reckoned only On the amount of capital advanced to pay the owner of that labour the natural price of his labour. What now is the proportion which the necessary labour for this purpose bears to the extra labour which is used for the benefit of the capitalist alone?

Nothing will illustrate this so clearly as actual figures taken from the regular operations of a factory. A mill with 10,000 spindles spins yarn No.32 with American cotton, and produces every week a pound of yarn to the spindle. The waste of the cotton amounts to six per cent. Therefore 10,600 pounds of cotton are each week converted into 10,000 pounds of yarn, and 600 pounds of waste. In April, 1871, this cotton cost 7¾d. a pound, and consequently £342 were paid for the 10,600 pounds, in round figures. The 10,000 spindles, including the spinning machines and the engine, cost to £10,000; their wear and tear amounts to ten per cent., or £1000 a year, or £20 a week. The ground-rent is £300 a year, or £6 a week. Coal costs £4 10s. every week gas, oil, &c.; the total weekly expenses in constant value amounting to £378.

The wages of the hands are £52 a week; the price of the yarn at 12¼d. a pound for 10,000 pounds is £510. The value produced each week is consequently £510-£378, or £132. Now deduct the variable capital, the wages of the hands, or £52, and there remains a surplus value of £80. Here the rate of surplus value is therefore as £80 to £52, or upwards of 153 per cent. That is to say, for an average day's work of ten hours the necessary labour is but four hours, and the extra labour six hours; or, the labourer works four hours for himself, and six for other people, who divide his extra work among them.

And yet how unreasonable that the "hand," silly fellow, should object to this division of his extra and unpaid for labour, and fancy that somehow somebody has got the better of him. Fool that he is, let him listen to the voice of the preacher and the political economist:– "What you need, my weary, poverty-stricken, Christian brother, is not to get back your own extra labour, which you have expended, in the form of money or goods for your own use. That is – believe us, who are your true friends – robbery of the capitalists. You, my good man, should be thrifty, abstinent, saving, economical, and still go on steadily providing extra labour for others, until you in turn cease to be a labourer, turn capitalist, and extort extra labour yourself."

What, however is this day's work, necessary labour and extra labour together, which the capitalist buys on the market? Obviously there must be some limit to it. A man can't work twenty-four hours on end every day in the week, that is clear. But the limits of the day's work are very elastic. We find ten hours, twelve hours, fourteen, sixteen, even eighteen hours, given as the amount of a day's work. And this limit, however loose already, capitalists, from the shirt-sweaters up to the railway companies, are always striving to extend. They invoke the sacred laws of supply and demand and freedom of contract, to sanction an amount of daily toil which leaves a man or a woman utterly exhausted at its close, which weakens health, reduces vitality, and hands on a broken constitution to the progeny. And all for what? In order to swell that surplus value which "society" depends upon for its excessive luxury and continuous laziness. "But," say the labourers when adjured not to endanger society, "that is all very well; but society is shamefully wronging us. It is society which, having entire command of the forces of the country, enables the capitalist class thus to violate every law of exchange with impunity. These are they who pay us only one-half or one-third or one-quarter of the real value of our day's work. They then are the people who are endangering society, of which we form by far the most important part – not the working men, who ask only that their labour should not be taken for nothing."

There is a comparison at hand which philanthropizing capitalists – and there are many of them – will understand, if they do not appreciate. Under the old system of *corvée* a man was obliged to give, say one day's work in the week, or at most two, to his lord without any payment. Such a man, though he had the remaining five or six days wholly to himself, was thought little better than a slave. Nor was he. English capitalists would, of all men, subscribe largely to relieve human beings from continuing in such a shameful and degraded position. But here at home, we have men, women, and children, who are obliged to give four, five, six hours a day to the capitalist for nothing, and yet are thought free. A factory hand who, as in the instance given above, provides six hours a day of extra labour, makes the capitalist a present of three days' work in the week for nothing. He gives, in fact, three times as much labour for nothing in the week to his employer, as the serf who works one day in the week under *corvée* is obliged to offer in unpaid labour to his lord. But in the one case, under the system of daily or weekly wages, the necessary labour and the extra labour are lumped together as so much paid-for labour; in the other, they are divided. Thus the forced, extra, unpaid labour for the capitalist – the industrial *corvée* – escapes notice, though it is

51

three times greater than the other, and the capitalist is thrice as heavy a master as the feudal lord.

Moreover, the capitalist class has ever been on the look-out to increase the hours of labour beyond measure, in order that they may obtain more extra labour, and thus secure more surplus value. We in England have had sad experience of the baneful effects upon the working population of the never-ceasing endeavours to increase the number of working hours. The reports of the Factory Inspectors up to a comparatively recent date, are positively filled to overflowing with instances of the efforts made by the capitalists to crowd extra labour on men, on women, and, above all, on children. A little is filched from the meal times; the mill is opened a trifle earlier, closed something later, than the prescribed hour. Always this persistent scheming for extra labour. [2] Not only up to the passing of the Factory Acts, but ever since, the same tendency has been relentlessly displayed. Free Trade, by reducing the natural price of labour, increased the profit of capitalists and the number of hours on which they could depend for the production of surplus value. Women and children have, of course, suffered fearfully. They were used up as so much food for surplus value, without the slightest regard to humanity, or to the interest of the country at large. The average age of the working classes was fearfully shortened by the excessive toil. The cotton industry of Lancashire alone in ninety years, or three generations of ordinary men, devoured nine generations of work-people. What mattered that to the manufacturers? There were more where they came from. The poor bargainers reproduce themselves, and supply and demand goes merrily on as before. The Factory Acts themselves, still by no means so stringent nor so rigidly administered as they ought to be, were carried against the bitterest opposition of the capitalist class, because the nation had gradually roused itself to the truth that the whole population was rapidly deteriorating, owing to the systematic overwork of women and children. There are even still economists of liberal views, who hold that women in particular ought to be allowed to work in factories as long as they choose, and that the State has no right to interfere to protect the coming generation. Argument after argument is put forward also that longer hours than those to which the Trade Unions have happily reduced the working day are essential, because otherwise capitalists cannot compete with foreign nations. [3]

There is, unfortunately, no need to go back to the horrible details contained in the Health Reports of a few years ago, as to the condition of the working classes, whilst wealth is being piled up by their labour all round them. In spite of a little permissive legislation – well-intended, but by no means effectual – things are almost as bad to-day. Some there are of course who, rejoicing in the fact that our population has consumed on the average 100lb. per head more of bacon in the last ten years, or .002 lb. per head more cheese, decline to look to that portion of the people who bring down the average.

Such a speech as that delivered by the Bishop of Manchester in June, 1880, ought to awaken the nation to the mischief which is still being done. He, worthy man, wrings his hands in despair at the state of affairs in his own diocese. People living in the most miserable poverty, from which there seems no escape. Misery, filth, starvation, overcrowding, followed by inevitable deterioration. Sadness and hopelessness brood over the streets, and alleys, and cellars, he has explored. What can education do with children living in such conditions as those which he has so graphically described? The men and the women too work hard enough when they can get the chance – work endless hours too – do enough in short to feed, and lodge, and clothe themselves in comfort. Yet in Manchester and Salford, in Stockport and Altrincham, in Oldham and Macclesfield, throughout the whole of these great industrial districts, thousands on thousands of labourers exist in good times in squalor, whilst bad times drive them at once to the wall. Dr.

Fraser himself had shown a few years before what the condition of the agricultural labourer was in this respect, how hard he too works, how little he gets, how foully he is lodged in many cases. Even orthodox economists show further how farmers and manufacturers alike combine to keep down the rate of wages to the bare natural price, or below it, whilst exacting the longest possible hours of toil.

Admitting that in some respects matters have improved, owing to the determination of the working classes no longer to submit to such neglect and oppression as of old, the very last report of the Factory inspectors shows how much remains to be done, and how little machinery there is to do it. The long weary struggle which has been carried on by the working class, without even proper representation, against *laissez-faire*, political economy, and selfish ideas of freedom, seems still far from being successful.

A mere list of the provisions of the Factory Acts to restrict tyranny by the masters and injury resulting to the hands, proves conclusively that, but for State intervention a condition of slavery of the worst kind would exist now, as it did forty years ago. Meals for instance are not allowed now to be taken in rooms where the atmosphere is poisonous, and some restrictions are even imposed upon keeping men, women, and children employed in the poisonous atmosphere. In Bradford, a city which has long lived in the full and rather greasy odour of Liberal sanctity, the wool-sorting has for years been carried on in such a manner as directly to involve the loss of the lives of many of the hands. Not a single improvement did the capitalists – Mr. Coercion-Bill Forster is a Bradford man – introduce, till forced to do so by law, and by public opinion following upon the verdict of coroners' juries as to the infamous state of things which brought about the death of the wool-sorters. Children still go to work full time in the collieries when they are twelve years old, though in factories they, fortunately, may not do so until they are thirteen or fourteen. The parents, eager to get their children's wages, take advantage of this, and the capitalist colliery owner of course is always ready to employ cheap child-labour for his engines or other purposes.

In the dangerous trades great improvements have been made by the Factory Acts, but still it is evident far more stringent inspection and regulation is required. In the brickworks we read of a girl carrying to and fro eleven tons of clay in the day for 2s. 3d. a day. Brickmaking, to which women are wholly unsuited, fell into their hands, we are told, "because masters at one time got wages down very low" wanted to work women on the cheap in fact. In the great cotton and iron industries years must still elapse before the people recover from the deteriorating effects of unrestricted competition. The best factories and ironworks are not yet controlled sufficiently in the interest of the men, women, and children who work in them. But those who wish to understand what capitalism is capable of, and what is its natural bait, should read the reports of the factory inspectors, Messrs. Lakeman and Gould, on the sweating system at the East End of London, and the dens in which the unfortunate milliners and dressmakers work at the West End. "Workshops," says Inspector Lakeman, "arc generally small, over-crowded, very dirty, overheated, badly ventilated; and when half a dozen gas burners are alight for five or six hours in a twelve-feet square room, one can imagine that the term 'sweater' is not inappropriate ... So gigantic has the sweating system become, so rapid the production (for the division of labour is strictly carried out), so varied are the wants of each occupier, that one despairs of making any impression upon these people except by compulsion. *They are bound to a system which excludes freedom,* and from long habit it seems impossible to move them out of it. Now when we see a cloth coat made, lined, braided by hand, the silk and thread found by sweater, all for 2s. 3d, and if the total number be not returned to the clothier completed by the time specified, then a fine of sixpence (I have seen one shilling) levied for each garment, one cannot wonder at the desire of the sweater to keep his team late at night to complete his task." Coats are sometimes "finished in this style," however, as low as 2s. "When one thinks that there are about 18,000 to 20,000 people toiling at this one trade of making ready-made clothing, can we wonder at beholding the palace-like premises of merchant tailors who can advertise garments at a very low price, which to them is the cost of material, and say 2s. 1d. for the making of a coat? It does not require much depth of reasoning to judge where the profit comes from." [4] No, worthy Mr. Inspector, it does not. The profit of the merchant tailor, like the profit of his noble allies the cotton lords and the wool factors, comes out of the unpaid labour of others, whom he throws upon the streets when they have served his turn of providing surplus value according to the universal law of supply and demand and freedom of contract.

But again; hear Mr. Inspector Gould:– "There is, however, one branch of work, giving employment to thousands of girls and women. which, although entirely harmless in itself, is yet, unfortunately, solely by reason of the conditions under which it is carried on, a typically unhealthy business, I need hardly say that I refer to the making of all articles of ladies' clothing, and principally to the dressmaking section of the trade. Of the thousands of young and delicate girls who are engaged in trying to earn a bare subsistence in a deleterious atmosphere, no one can tell how many go down in the struggle. No statistics can be formed of the percentage of deaths, of enfeebled constitutions, of the amount of disease engendered in the first instance by the deadly atmosphere of the workrooms in second and third class establishments devoted to the dressmaking and ladies' clothing trade in the West End of London. I know of no class of female workers whose vital interests are so entirely neglected, and who labour under such disadvantageous conditions, as the unlucky victims of the dressmaking industry. Nothing is more surprising than to hear the advocates of 'women's rights' of both sexes, in full knowledge apparently of the hardships undergone by the very class whose battle they profess to fight, cry out for absolute liberty of action to all females employed in labour!" Evidently Mr. Gould is quite ignorant of the real bigotry of the advocates of freedom, and had better look to himself. In the shops themselves things are little better. Men and women are kept at work from thirteen to fourteen hours a day for five days in the week, and for sixteen hours on the sixth day.

As to the accommodation of the labouring class, out of whose unpaid toil the capitalist makes his profit and society waxes fat, the Reports on Artisans' Dwellings, give deplorable facts. Two and three families pigged together into one or two small rooms; streets of houses torn down for improvements, and their occupiers forced to crowd in upon the already overcrowded streets adjoining. This is the rule throughout all our great cities. London is no worse than Glasgow, nor Glasgow worse than Birmingham, Bradford, Leeds, Manchester, or Newcastle. The latter city, indeed, is perhaps the worst of all in this respect in comparison to its population. Hitherto the mere Permissive Acts to remedy this state of things have been almost useless. Yet the homes of the poor are not cheap; they are dear. Cubic space for cubic space, the dens of the East and West End cost more than the mansions of the rich, who have good air, good light, plentiful supply of water, and all that's needed for healthy existence. Those who provide them with all these benefits are left to take care of themselves. No compulsion: that would be too serious. What? force the municipalities to tear down foul, unhealthy dwellings, at the expense of the rich, and build up proper accommodation for the poor? Never," say the ratepayers; "that would touch us: it is communism, confiscation, the overturn of society."

We are now in cycle of rising prosperity for the moneyed and manufacturing class. Now is their opportunity to endeavour to remedy in their turn too some of the mischiefs below and around them. They justly denounce the selfishness of landlords; let them, too, look at home. But the working class should rely on their own power and peaceful strength – they must trust to themselves alone. To them, then, I say:– All wealth is produced by labour, and goods exchange in proportion to the quantity of human labour which is embodied in them. Between the workers of all civilized countries there is no real difference: they create the wealth and produce the food, and, under proper conditions, all would live in moderation all would have enough. But landowners, capitalists, merchants, money-lenders, have possessed themselves of the land, of the machinery, of the currency, of the credit. They therefore compel the workman to labour long and live hardly for their benefit; they take of the time, and the life, and the labour of their fellows for nothing. Those who own the soil, and those who manufacture – those who live on interest, and those who trade on differences of value, live alike in luxury and in idleness out of the sweat and the misery of others. They, therefore, are the enemies of the great mass of the people, to be overcome by voluntary combination and peaceful endeavour. You, then, who produce the wealth in every country, consider where you stand; you, men who have seen your homes broken up, your health destroyed, and have beheld your wives and children fade away under the tyranny of capitalism, stop and think. Let all who are made poor and miserable for the advantage of others, take heed to themselves. And having thus considered, thus thought, and thus looked at home, stretch out your hands, now powerless, to the workmen of the world as your friends, and begin a new and better social epoch for humanity. Working men and working women of Great Britain and Ireland, who now toil and suffer that others may be lazy and rich – Unite! Working men and working women of Europe and America, who now rejoice in the gleam of a transient prosperity, only to be cast into deeper despair on the next stagnation – Unite! Unite! In union alone is safety and happiness for the future, as in difference and selfishness have been danger and misery in the past. Therefore, once more, working men and working women, ye who live hardly to day, to pass on sadness and poverty to your children tomorrow, Unite! Unite! Unite!

Notes

1. Professor Stanley Jevons has convinced himself that labour has no influence on value. Utility is the sole source of value. Labour, supply, utility – such is the progression. This is not the place to discuss this theory, which is of course turned to account at once by capitalists. The cloud of differentiations and metaphysics which Mr. Jevons throws up as he goes along does not, however, obscure the fact that without labour there would be no value at all.

2. Mr. Watherston, a jeweller, who has grown rich on other men's labour, wrote not long ago to the **Economist** to complain of the miserably short hours of work Englishmen now have. They must work more, or trade – his profits, he meant – would suffer. Of course this was the very man for the capitalist party. They got him at once as chairman of the Westminster caucus. How long will working men be gulled by landlords and capitalists into providing them with more unpaid labour, under the pretence of improving trade?

3. To show how impossible it is for the capitalist class to shake themselves clear of the prejudices in which they have been brought up, it is almost enough to say that Mr. Bright – a man surely distinguished for his humanity in general concerns – opposed the Factory Acts, which may fairly be regarded as the most beneficent measures of this century, with all his might; that when President of the Board of Trade he declared that adulteration was a legitimate form of competition; and that to this hour he cannot see that interference with freedom of contract as between the capitalist and the labourer may be absolutely essential in the interests of the community at large. Mr. Thomas Brassey, as Professor Cairnes has pointed out, could not understand that a reduction of profits might be quite as desirable as a reduction of wages. It is amusing, too, to see it capitalist who has taken £700,000 out of the working classes by extra labour, and owns a rigid monopoly, posing as a leader of the democracy. Doubtless they all think themselves thoroughly in earnest; but *how can* hunters alter surplus value, men who are every day engaged in putting wages at a lower level than they ought to be in order to enhance their own profits from unpaid labour, really lead or benefit them by pretending to lead, the working class The Liberal benches in the House of Commons at this very time are closely packed with plutocrats, who have made all their wealth, and mean to make more, Out of the unpaid labour of their own countrymen. The Conservative benches seat a growing proportion of men of the like kidney. What wonder that working men who really understand what is going on around therm almost despair of success in carrying measures which are absolutely essential to tlie welfare of their class, when the power of capitalism is increasing in every direction, when there is not single daily newspaper in existence which represents their interests or advocates their claims, and when only three of their class sit in Parliament?

4. Lord Salisbury spoke at the Merchant Tailors' Hall not long since, of the absurdity of "plate-hunger." It seemed more ridiculous to his aristocratic mind than even the earth-hunger of the Irish. Had he by chance a Conservative sweater at his elbow?

59

Chapter III Capital

Capital is the produce of past labour devoted to present production. "The wealth which has been accumulated with the object of assisting production, is termed capital; and therefore the capital of the country is the wealth which is not immediately consumed unproductively, and which may consequently be devoted to assist the further production." Capital is in fact the saving of past labour, for the special purpose of increasing the future store. Undoubtedly capital originally may have been acquired by saving or by inheritance, though that is only pushing the accumulation a step further back; and the grain pits of Northern India, the yarn barrows and tabu cocoa-nut groves of Polynesia, the stores of the Mexican aborigines, represent early and useful forms of capital. "Nothing," says Mr. Fawcett, "more distinctly marks the superiority of man over the brute creation than the prudent foresight which causes an adequate provision to be made for the future. The more civilized men are, the more is this foresight shown. Civilized men anticipate with keen perception the wants of the future. To provide against the contingencies of the future, engrosses perhaps the too anxious care of the nation."

In these sentences Mr. Fawcett expresses far too favourable a view of the foresight of the present generation of civilized men. Never perhaps since civilization was first seen on the planet, have so many human beings been passing through life at the same time on insufficient food, as at the present moment. Nothing, indeed, is more striking than the want of foresight displayed under our present capitalist system of production. Whichever quarter of the globe we look to, we see the future entirely disregarded. We in England, for example, a vast industrial community, are content to base our supplies more and more upon countries thousands of miles from our shores.

America, which affords us our chief quantity of food, is using up wheat centre after wheat centre in a fashion similar to that not long since in vogue in South Australia; forests, which can perhaps never be replaced, are swept away, in every direction, to the permanent injury of the climate. In England, manure to the value of at least £25,000,000 a year, is sent down into the sea, though our soil is deteriorating for want of it. Foresight, therefore, in any extended sense, cannot certainly be claimed for our existing civilization, unless the Romans showed foresight when they worked out the Campagna to ruin, and destroyed the future of Sicily by their exactions. What capital has done for India I shall show later on; what it would do, if left unrestrained, for our own people has been seen, in part, in the last chapter. But granting that the capital which begins work is the result of past frugality on the part of some hard-working man with a keen eye to the good of his species, as well as to his own immediate interest, what is the next capital, and the next, and the next, which rolls up so rapidly in this island of ours? Let us go back to the great cotton industry once more, and look about us there.

A man has a capital of say £10,000, inherited from his thrifty parent, who bequeathed it to him after a long life of usefulness, with many prayers that he would make it fructify. He does. Four-fifths he devotes to buying machinery, raw cotton, &c., and one-fifth he expends in wages. Every year he produces 240,000 pounds of cotton yarn of the value of £12,000. His £10,000 has been reproduced, and his surplus value is in the 40,000 pounds of yarn, which are sold for the sum of £2,000. This £2,000 of surplus value forms a new capital, which, when set to work in like manner, will produce in its turn a surplus value of £400 – and so on, and so on, as may seem convenient to the capitalist. The original £10,000 came from the pious parent, but the history of the new capital of the £2,000, of the £400 &c., stares us in the face. It is simply surplus value, other people's unpaid extra labour, capitalized.

The means of production in which this additional extra labour is embodied, as well as the means which support it, are only portions of the tribute levied every year from the working class by the capitalist class. It is, of course, perfectly in accordance with the economical laws which govern the production of commodities, and with the ever sacred rights of property which follow thereupon. Nevertheless there are the following results:–

1. That the product belongs to the capitalist, and not to the producer.

2. That the value of this product includes both the value of the capital and the surplus value, which costs the workmen labour, but the capitalist whose lawful property it becomes, nothing.

3. That the labourer has kept up his force of labour and can sell it again on the market, if he is lucky enough to find a buyer.

Thus capital rolls up by crystallizing unpaid labour in the hands of the capitalist.

That the general position of the modern labourer in dealing with his master the capitalist is bad enough, has been shown only too clearly. Whenever the Government slackens its intervention for a moment, even with existing Factory Acts in full force, the employers, as a class, strive their utmost to extend the hours of labour, and thus to get more unpaid work out of their hands. Not the slightest regard is paid to the health or well-being of the men, women, and children whose lives are used up thus relentlessly; the truck system, which filches wages, is resorted to wherever possible; and adulteration has become the rule rather than the exception in trade. To increase the rate of surplus value produced per head employed is of course a great gain; the average amount of profit on the variable capital used is at once increased likewise. Who can wonder then that having the control of the powers of the country, and the recognized political economists as their submissive fuglemen, the capitalist class should so long have ridden roughshod over the working class in the name of freedom?

In considering, however, the origin of the capitalist system, it becomes clear that without a minimum amount of variable capital wherewith to pay wages, that mode of production cannot soon begin. A man who works for himself alone, need work only the eight hours which we may assume to be required, on the average, to provide him with the necessaries of subsistence. He would need then only the means of production for his eight hours' work; whilst the capitalist, who makes him work an extra four hours, needs an additional sum of money to provide the means of production for those four hours. Moreover, the capitalist, even if he lived no better than the workmen he employed, would have to keep two of them at work for twelve hours a day, in order that he himself might have the necessaries of life in idleness. Even so there would be no surplus wealth. So that. according to this calculation, the lazy capitalist, in order to be able to live without work even twice as well as his workmen, and turn into capital half the surplus value produced, must advance eight times the amount of capital required for a single independent workman, though only four hands will be employed in producing surplus value. This done, capital at once becomes master of the situation. The workman no longer turns the means of production to account, but they turn him to account, and work up his force of labour into surplus value to an extent which has never been brought about under any system of forced labour known to history.

The history of the development of capitalist production, from simple cooperation and manufacture up to the present preponderance of the great machine industries, shows an enormous growth of wealth for the capitalist class, combined with steady pressure upon the labourer to produce more surplus value by low wages and overwork. At first the true capitalist method scarcely makes head; but when once labourers are collected together in one building, to do separate tasks at the bidding of an employer, they cease to be separate individuals, and become an organism, bound to exercise their collective capacity in accordance with the rules of capital. Here comes in that minute division of manual labour, so advantageous to production, which has been described with so much enthusiasm by many economists. The object of the collection of the labourers together was, of course, to cheapen the production of merchandise. The extra ability which the workman derives from devoting his attention to one operation instead of to several, the time saved by the juxtaposition of the labourers, &c., all tell in favour of the capitalist, whose interest is henceforth exclusively consulted. For the labourer has already become a mere tool. He no longer produces commodities himself, as he did before, but embodies his work in bits of commodities, or in helping to make a complete commodity, only valuable when put together. To carry on perpetually one petty operation in a complicated whole, working day in and day out to produce surplus value for the capitalist by a series of purely mechanical operations, such is the labourer's portion in this system of manufacture. He still seems to be an independent agent working with his own tools, but this is precisely what in reality he is not.

Glass-making, watch-making, pin-making, and other trades, are still to a great extent conducted on this transition method, and afford illustrations of what was not long since general. Whilst then the social division of labour, with or without the exchange of commodities, belongs to the economical forms of most various societies, the manufacturing division of labour is the special creation of the capitalist system of production. The workshop is in fact a machine, of which the parts are human beings. Dissociate the individuals from the machine as a whole, and they become almost as useless as a crank, a pin, or an eccentric, detached from a steam-engine. The labourer, to start with, sells his force of labour to capital because he is destitute of the means of production himself; now his labour has become absolutely useless unless it is sold. He can work henceforth to advantage only in the workshop of the capitalist. It is also the tendency of manufacture thus conducted to employ more and more hands as capital accumulates and the minimum of capital needed to commence, increases.

This sort of co-operation was a historical necessity, in order to convert isolated labour into social work. It begins about the middle of the sixteenth century, and lasts to the latter half of the eighteenth century, as the chief method of production in capitalist countries. During the whole of this period, and far on into the nineteenth century, the most atrocious laws were enacted by the small minority of the population who owned the Houses of Parliament, against the increase of wages, or any combination on the part of the working classes to secure for themselves justice and consideration. Capitalists might combine at their pleasure; employers might break their contract at will; but, woe betide those unlucky workmen who thought that freedom meant the right to strike to get better wages, or to step out of a contract which imperilled their health. For them the prison, flogging, branding, forced labour at the filthiest tasks. But for the capitalist? – he went on his way rejoicing, with more and yet more of other men's labour at his mercy, and in due course of time he "founded a family," figured as an Abolitionist, and died in the odour of sanctity.

Steam machinery gave a new turn to the screw which pressed down the working class, and began those periods of inflation and stagnation, of over-production and depression, which many have come to regard as inevitable accompaniments of all production. The machine sprang naturally out of manufacture, but the use of steam as a motive power gave it a development in many directions which could never have been obtained in any other way. At first sight it would appear that machines must of necessity improve the lot of the bulk of mankind – that as they so vastly enhance the productive power

66

of human labour, men would be relieved from excessive drudgery, and yet wealth would abound more than at any previous period.

This was the view of the ancients. Aristotle foresaw that slavery could be done away if machines were invented; and others have dreamed of a state of society where, by their help, the history of the people should cease to be one of perpetual poverty and degradation. As machines save labour alike in agriculture and in working up the raw material, there is nothing necessarily chimerical in such ideas. But capital has stepped in and taken order with these vain imaginings. The riches due to machinery have gone to the few: the many have become mere slaves to the machine. For that is the result: human beings no longer make use of their implements; they themselves are made to serve the machine.

The machine of course, though it increases the productive power of the human labour employed, adds no more value to the commodity produced than the wear and tear during the process of work. But the first effect of its introduction is to bring into competition with adult male labour that of women and children, who could, and do, serve machines as well as the superior force of the men, and serve also to reduce their wages – the main object of the capitalist. But another advantage is afforded by the machine to the employer. We have seen that the profit of the capitalist depends upon the amount of unpaid labour he can exact from the free workman. In ordinary circumstances this can only be increased by the lengthening of the hours of labour. But by the aid of machines the labour can be intensified as well as prolonged. Thus a man may produce the necessary amount of labour-value in a shorter period, and leave a larger portion of the working day as surplus value to his employer, by an improvement in machinery which renders the labour rapid and severe. Ever since the law stepped in to shorten the hours of labour for women and children, and men combined to shorten their own hours, the endeavour to intensify labour by increasing the rapidity of machines has been unceasing. This has produced in the cotton and silk factories a state of nervous excitement among the workers which has greatly augmented the proportion of chest complaints. Twelve hours' work are now compressed into ten hours. This work, too, is of the most monotonous, uninteresting character. In return for that exhausting labour the working classes as a body suffer as the Bishop of Manchester has so graphically described.

But the effect of the introduction of new machines of greatly improved capacity, used not for the benefit of the whole community, but primarily for that of the dominant class, has a far more serious influence upon the working class than even the competition of women and children which it admits of, or the intensity of labour which results therefrom. A new labour-saving machine means so much labour thrown upon the market without the means of earning subsistence. This effect of improved machinery is admitted by Ricardo, who, after having previously held the contrary opinion, satisfied himself "that the substitution of machinery for human labour is often very injurious to the class of labourers." This view is taken less clearly by Macculloch, and Mill, and Fawcett; but they contend that the compensations are rapid, and in the end beneficial. The labouring classes, according to them, are therefore benefited, not injured, by the introduction of improved machinery in every case. The labourers whom the machine displaces are nevertheless thrown upon the market, where they certainly increase the amount of labour available for the capitalist. This is in itself a terrible matter for them all. But the amount of capital invested in the machine ceases also to be available for wages; and if the machine works up an increased amount of raw material with far fewer hands, the constant capital is clearly greatly augmented at the expense of the variable, or that which is immediately available for the payment of wages. The men thus thrown out of work are good for very little in other employments, and consequently fall to a lower grade. If they get fresh work in the same trade, that is owing to the introduction of some new capital, not certainly to that which is, already locked up in the machine, and employed in obtaining food for it in the shape of raw materials. The machine itself has nothing to do with the sad effect produced. The result of its employment is that the product is cheaper and more abundant than ever before; yet the workman is thrown aside into penury, and the capitalist pursues his triumphant career. For this temporary inconvenience is now of perpetual recurrence; and the fate of the miserable hand-loom weavers of India, starved in the interests of Manchester manufacturers, is reproduced in a milder form among the labourers whose interests these very cotton-lords were pretending to serve. The necessary influence of the machine under present conditions is to place the labourers at an increasing disadvantage – a disadvantage which they can never overcome, save by political and social combinations and rearrangements, carried out with steadfastness and zeal for at least a generation.

For this brings the question home to that miserable see-saw of inflation and depression to that sad condition of the mass of the labouring poor in the ever-growing population of our great cities, to which reference has so often been made. "Oh yes," say the followers of Malthus, by no means confined to Mr. Bradlaugh and Mrs. Besant, "but this over-population is at the root of the whole mischief. If only the working class would keep itself under restraint, and not breed at such a terrible pace, they would at once raise their wages by the eternal law of supply and demand. They have to thank their own early marriages and excessive birth-rate for much of their present misery."

Is this so? The evidence is really all the other way. There is nothing whatever to show that these islands are overpeopled in proportion to the wealth that is being accumulated. Very much the contrary. The population of Great Britain and Ireland has doubled in the last seventy years. It is now increasing at the rate of about one-and-a-half per cent. in every ten years. But the riches, the income, the accumulations of the country, are they increasing at a less rate so that abstention from marriage and Malthusian devices are so essential? Why, it is notorious to all that our wealth has increased out of all calculable proportion to our population during the present century. The whole world is laid under contribution, to furnish additional wealth for the exported savings of unpaid labour made by the comfortable classes here at home. English capital brings back its return from all quarters of the globe; whilst in these islands, the comparison between what was and what is, can scarcely be expressed in sober language. Nay, even during this late period of prolonged depression, when the hard, rough men of the iron districts, as well as the distressed cotton-spinners and miners, were declaring that they would not go into the workhouse, and yet could not "clem" for another winter – even in those hardest of hard times, it was calculated by an expert that in addition to ordinary investments, which were going on all the time, no less than £250,000,000 were watching the opportunity to be laid out to a profit when, to use the cant phrase, business once more recovered. Whilst population is now increasing at the rate of one-and-a-half per cent. in every ten years, capital and wealth squandered in luxury are rolling up at the rate of ten, twenty, thirty per cent. per annum.

A few figures will make this quite clear. Taking the years 1848 and 1878, the period of one generation since last there was an agitation in favour of justice to the multitude, we find that the total gross annual value of property and profits assessed to Income Tax in Great Britain and Ireland – about half the actual gross annual value, or less – was in round figures £275,000,000 in 1848, against £578,000,000, in 1878, or an increase *on assessment for income alone* of upwards of 110 per cent. in the thirty years. A truly enormous increase. Yet the total population in 1848 was 28,000,000, as against nearly 34,000,000 in 1878. Here, then in the United Kingdom, an increase of the annual assessed income of 110 per cent. or of £303,000,000, since 1848, has been accompanied by an increase in the population of only 6,000,000, or at the rate of less than twenty per cent. in the thirty years.

What fatal nonsense then is it to talk of overpopulation in such a case as this. If the increased capital had been used for the benefit of all, then these extra 6,000,000, as well as the 28,000,000, would have been living in comfort, health, and well-being – well-housed, well-clothed, well-fed, well-educated. The over-population which the Malthusians think to check by their wrong and mistaken methods, is due to the special system of production under which we groan, and will continue so long as, and no longer than, it is brought under restraint for the advantage of all. It is the deprivation of the means of selling their labour on fair terms that does the mischief to the mass of the population. Let the people remember, that if no one were overworked in this free land of ours, there would not at this moment be hands enough in the country to carry on its business – that if only one-half of the livers in luxury and idleness on the excessive labour of others turned to some higher ideal of patriotism, there would be plenty for all. It is not the population that crowds on the means of subsistence, but the concentration of the produce of their toil in so few hands, that is obnoxious; though the way out to a better and fairer distribution is not so simple as some of the easy handlers of the complicated machinery of our modern society would imagine.

This over-population then, which occasions such sad scenes in times of depression, and is ever close at hand in the flushest days of trade, is not actual but relative, and is directly due to the employment of machines and the growing proportion of constant to variable capital. Natural causes – great famines in the East, serious wars in Europe, short harvests at home, may aggravate the depression, as sloth and unthriftiness add to the misfortunes of the working class. But such decennial crises as those now observable date from the present century, and owe their development to the circumstances stated.

The reproduction of capital necessarily carries with it the simultaneous reproduction of the source of surplus value – force of labour. Accumulation of capital is at the same time increase of the mere wage-earning class. And the payment of wages presupposes that a certain amount of labour is given for nothing. Wages, therefore, can only rise because there is an increase of capital in excess of the labour offered. Yet the rise of wages and consequent diminution of unpaid labour does not mean that the domain of capitalism is restricted; the small profits only necessitate bigger capitals, and the workman sees in the wealth of his master his only hope of safety. Or on the other hand, the rate of wages retards the amount of accumulation, and then the excessive amount of capital seeking employment in comparison to the labour on offer – and then wages fall to the level which suits the views of capital. Thus the see-saw goes on. Now an excess of capital arising from accelerated accumulation, which renders the labour on offer insufficient and raises its price; again a slackened accumulation makes the labour on offer relatively excessive and reduces its price. All this has nothing to do with the increase and decrease of population, but may occur, and does occur, when the population is stationary.

The real law of capitalist production is this:- The relation between the accumulation of capital and the rate of wages is only a relation between unpaid labour converted into capital and the overplus of paid labour that this additional capital needs in order to set to work. This then is not a relation between two matters quite independent of one another – that is to say, on the one side the magnitude of the capital, on the other the number of the working population; but a relation only *between the paid and the unpaid labour of the same working population.* If the quantity of unpaid labour which the working class supplies and the capitalist class accumulates increases with sufficient rapidity for its conversion into additional capital to necessitate an extraordinary addition to the quantity of paid labour, wages rise. Other things remaining the same, unpaid labour diminishes in proportion. So soon, however, as this diminution reaches the point when the extra labour which furnishes the additional capital is no longer forthcoming in the usual quantity, a reaction ensues. A less part of the return is converted into capital, and the rise of wages is checked. Thus – and this is the point of most serious import to the working classes of this country – the price of labour can never rise except between limits which leave quite untouched the groundwork of the capitalist system and ensure the reproduction of capital on a progressive scale. Never then until the working class shake themselves clear of the notion that a mere rise of wages is all they have to strive for, will they be able to control the capitalist class. The labourer is thus really the slave of his own production in existing economical conditions.

For, as has been stated more than once, the demand for labour is occasioned, not by the actual amount of capital but by that of its variable portion, which alone employs labour. But the magnitude of this portion relatively to the whole is constantly decreasing. At times, however, the conversion of variable into constant capital is less felt, machines are introduced less frequently. Then there arises that greater demand for labour which under ordinary conditions follows upon the accumulation of capital. But at the very moment when the number of the workmen employed by the capital reaches its maximum, there is such a glut of produce that at the slightest check in disposing of the goods the whole social machinery seems to come to a dead stop, the discharge of workmen comes suddenly on a vast scale and in a violent manner, and the very upset forces capitalists to excessive efforts to economize labour. Improved machinery is introduced again, and the wheel works round.

Thus the tendency of our system of production and the increasing accumulation of capital, is to increase at the same time the amount of the over-population relatively to the means of employment. An industrial army of reserve is maintained of increasing dimensions, ever at the disposal of capital, ready to be absorbed during times of expansion, only to be thrown back in periods of collapse. Only under the control of the great industrial movement of our time, does the production of a superfluous population become a definite means for the development of wealth. During periods of stagnation this industrial army of reserve presses on the army in active employment to restrain its demands, when at length comes the period of over-production and great apparent prosperity. Thus, then, the law according to which an ever-increasing mass of riches can be produced with a less and still lessening expenditure of human force – this law which enables man as a social being to produce more and more with less labour, is turned by our capitalist system – where the means of production are not at the service of the labourer, but the labourer at the mercy of his means of production – directly to his disadvantage. As a direct consequence, the more power and resources placed at the command of labour, and the greater the competition of labourers for means of employment, the more precarious becomes the condition of the wage-earner, and his opportunities of selling his labour. The productive population is always increasing in a more rapid ratio than the capital has need of it.

All recent events do but serve to exhibit the general truth of this in more striking shape. Look at the movement of population; take note of the operation of strikes; observe the world-wide effect of crises at the present time: how the numbers of those who live from hand to mouth, or minister as domestic servants to the luxuries of the comfortable classes, grow in proportion to the rest of the population; how the strikes invariably fail on a falling market, and often leave the workmen in a worse condition than they were before they began; how, when a crisis begins in Vienna it is felt at once through the world, to the United States, and we see, even in that great territory 3,000,000 of tramps, without house or home, wandering through the country, exposed to the most furious laws enacted by the well-to-do, and waiting till capital shall be good enough to employ them again, and again turn them adrift; how we ourselves. discovered that the capitalized unpaid labour taken from our people to lend to rotten States, like San Domingo, Honduras, Paraguay, and Peru, had merely brought about here at home a fictitious industrial prosperity, to be followed by the longest, and for the mass of the working people the most trying, crisis known in recent times; how – but it is needless to go further; the facts, the bare hard facts, condemn unceasingly our unregulated system of capitalist production, which, based solely on selfishness and gratifying greed, takes no account of the morrow, nor any note whatever of the mischief inflicted on the human race. Where the State has interfered to control and change the baleful conditions of life for the mass of our countrymen, there, and there alone, has some little good been done.

What then, say the let-alone school, would you stop the operation of machinery, throw back the evolution of the race, and return to the natural savage for a reorganization of modern society? They who ask such questions are as silly as those who think all attempts to change our social organization must be necessarily traced to the French Revolution, and that those who, like myself, are determined to modify existing political and social conditions, must wish and strive for a general overturn. It is not so. But the working of capital is essentially immoral. It moves on irrespective of all human considerations, save the accumulation of wealth and the provision for ease and luxury. For fifty years England has been under the domination of the classes who live and trade upon unpaid labour. Surely it is high time that those people who provide it should be heard in their turn as to the system which weighs them down. To expect that the nation will at once abandon its idea of fancied individual freedom, in favour of a real collective freedom which shall consult and care for the interests of all, is a chimera. But seeing, as we cannot but see, the plain economical basis of so much of the misery all deplore, is it not reasonable that more rapid steps should be made in the direction of general improvement? So far all the sacrifices have been made by the working class. What they in their turn may rightfully demand at once as reasonable and practicable remedies for some portion of their ills, are:–

1. A curtailment of the hours of labour, eight hours being the working day.

2. Free and compulsory education in its widest sense.

3. A compulsory construction by the municipalities and county assemblies of fitting dwellings for the working classes, including a good and free supply of light, air, and water, and garden-ground where possible.

4. Really cheap transport, so that artisans may live at a distance from their work without incurring heavy expenditure.

Such social reforms would produce an effect more speedily than might be supposed; and the expenditure would be far more than repaid to the community at large by the increased physical strength, the superior intelligence and morality, and the greatly enhanced patriotism, in its best sense, of the mass of the community. That these changes would check the fearful crises consequent upon the capitalist system of production is nowise probable; but they would lead the way gradually to a better system, when all might enter more fully upon their duties to the whole country.

Men who are now deprived of the fruits of their labour, who live under bad social conditions, who are forced to resort to stamped work and adulterated manufacture in order that their employers may make a profit, would feel very differently if for their honest labour invested in sound goods they could obtain a rightful return themselves. The magic of property could then be felt in the general as well as the individual improvement. That industry will always have the better of laziness, that thrift must be more beneficial than extravagance, are truths which no political or social changes can shake. But as we stand, our laws and customs are directly calculated to foster excessive wealth on the one side and miserable poverty on the other. What wonder that the people should begin to ask themselves the why and the wherefore of all this disparity between the men who work and those who use them? None are more ready to pay for mental toil than those who work with their hands, none more ready to give up a portion of their labour for the benefit of their fellows. Now, however, the perpetual conflict of wages, the strife with capital, where the possibility of final success is pushed farther and farther into the distance, necessarily blunts that feeling of national greatness in the best sense which does so much to sweep away, even as it is, the meanness engendered by mere narrowness and greed. Those who are never certain of continuous employment, and have little time left for education, might well be pardoned if they thought only of their own selfish interests. That in the mass they do not do so, is the best hope for the future.

But in coming changes it behoves us to be careful, lest, in getting rid of the excessive influence of one dominant class, we do but strengthen the power of a meaner and a worse one in its place. If possession of land – as all reformers agree – should be regulated in the interests of the country in time to come, so also must capital, machinery, and the national highways. Conservatism has come to mean the dominance of landowners: Liberalism has been degraded to the service of capitalists. There is little perhaps to choose; but for the people it is to the full as important in the future that capital should be controlled as the land. Mere destruction for its own sake – anarchy, where the demon of Socialism may take the foremost and the hindmost together – is not in accordance with the views of Englishmen. To pull down a system, however bad, they must see that something is ready to take its place. The infinite mischiefs of capitalism must be removed as a better method of production grows up from below. We have sad experience that our so called individual liberty means too often only the development of monopoly and the tyranny of wealth. But that faculty of organization, that ingenuity in turning science and invention to account, may as well be used in the service of the many as to the selfish gratification of personal desires. There is room enough for the use of the highest powers, without the perpetual money-getting now in the ascendant. No man can live out of the current of his age; but it is time that a higher ideal were placed before the nation, and that the common sense of the community at large should save the next generation from the power of oppression now accorded to a system which develops in those who handle it neither foresight, patriotism, nor honesty. The very tendency of capital itself renders this essential. Each year sees it rolling up into larger and larger masses. The great joint-stock enterprises, where enormous capital is obtained from many contributors, gradually crush out smaller houses; large emporiums undersell small; large factories dwarf smaller. With. this increase too, the personal relation between employers and employed ceases, and powerful corporations begin to assert themselves as a political influence solely for selfish ends, and with the cold persistence and disregard for human interests which such associations invariably display. England, the greatest capitalist country, may well show the world how to take order with this dangerous growth that threatens to overshadow human progress, and regulate without injustice those purely selfish motives which hitherto have been looked to as the sole hope of advance in civilization.

Chapter IV Organization

Now does any one imagine that with our present restricted suffrage we are likely to carry in town or country the social changes absolutely essential for the well-being of the majority, or to reorganize our political machinery in a workable shape within a reasonable time? Those who think thus must be of a very sanguine disposition. When in history did classes who hold property and power give up any portion of their valuable and lucrative monopolies until they saw clearly that surrender would be less harmful than defeat? The natural inclination of so-called Conservatism is to make a dead stand against all reform; and only now and then does a man arise in any country who can persuade the people in possession that, if they wish to avoid an overturn, they must have a distinct constructive policy of their own.

Yet it is true that mere extension of the suffrage by itself does not suffice to bring about much beneficial change. In France manhood suffrage imposed upon the people the rule of Napoleon III, and his gang of gamblers and political thimble-riggers for twenty years. The master may have meant well enough in his way, but his men and their mistresses looked upon France as their fair prey. In Germany, as we see, universal suffrage has not prevented Prince Bismarck from maintaining the dominance of military Junkerdom over a well-educated and, in the main, peaceful people. In America the injurious influence of great capitalists is severely felt, though there the people have the power to put an end to their tyranny at once by combination at the polls. Even here in England we may observe the same slow action on the part of voters to bring forward social grievances. Wonders, for instance, were looked for from the Reform Bill of 1832. It would be quite amusing, if it were not a little sad, to read in the writers of the first quarter of this century what changes for the better would be made so soon as rotten boroughs were swept away, and the power of aristocrats shaken. Yet all this enthusiasm notwithstanding, fourteen years elapsed before even the Corn Laws were repealed – and that was a capitalist not a working-class measure, inasmuch as cheap food kept wages lower; and the Factory Acts were not passed, in a shape to be of any service, for sixteen years. Then, too, the man who did more than any other to force them on the legislature, in the face of the interested opposition of the capitalists, was a non-political aristocrat, the present Lord Shaftesbury.

So with the Reform Bill of 1867, which in the eyes of such a man as Mr. Lowe involved nothing short of revolution. What great measures for the advantage of the community at large have yet resulted from that? Ireland, no doubt, has secured some attention; and the School Boards have commenced the work of education; but on the whole it is surprising how little has been achieved in fourteen years. Still, it is impossible to doubt that pressure from without would assume a very different shape if every man in the British Islands not a felon were entitled to a vote. It is fair to assume that no further change is pressed on now with vigour, because the mass of the present voters have got all they want.

For though it is the fashion to say that the Reform Bill of 1867 gave power to the democracy, there is little evidence of that as yet. To this day the working class is outvoted by the shopkeeping class; and the preposterous absurdity of three-cornered constituencies has been foisted on us by political theorists, to make matters worse. The extension of the borough franchise to the counties will, no doubt, make a difference to the agricultural labourer, and facilitate the dealing with the land; but that only puts the increasing working class in the towns at a greater relative disadvantage. Manhood suffrage is really the only logical outcome of any arguments in favour of the extension of the suffrage at all. Those who make the wealth of the country have the right, if anybody has, to vote as to how it should be governed. Drawbacks to such an extension there are, of course; and elsewhere, as has been already remarked, mere universal suffrage has not secured the social advancement which might have been hoped for. But unless those who suffer most under present arrangements have at least the means of putting forward representatives definitely pledged beforehand to redress their grievances, the very motive power for reform is lacking alike in Parliament and in local assemblies. We are now in a vicious circle. Shut men out from voting, and a minority unjustly controls the country: give the vote to all, and there is the risk of wholesale corruption, as well as that ignorance should become the ultimate court of appeal.

What probability is there, however, that, under any circumstances, free compulsory education to remedy this ignorance – or the enactment that bribery shall be felony, to put a stop to corruption – will be carried in our existing Parliament with the present suffrage? The idea is by no means confined to the Conservatives that universal education must involve a very inconvenient growth of independence, which will render men and women disinclined to supply menial positions in the old-fashioned way. Possibly, too, the workers of the community would begin to inquire into the reasons of the present excessive disparity of wealth, which would be more inconvenient still. School Boards are already too expensive for some. The contention that really complete education is the duty of the State for the protection of the common interest, is looked upon as little short of socialism by the well-to-do, who of course wish their children to start lightly handicapped with a good education in the race of life. The old hierarchical notions indeed still go on, and people who have to fill the lower stations ought to be mere animals, without too much knowledge to make them anxious for higher things. In this matter England is still far behind countries which in respect of political intelligence and political training are greatly our inferiors. We who have hitherto led the way in so many European improvements, need not surely look any longer across the sea to find that Frenchmen and Germans have more share in the government of their country than ourselves. More than ever important is it then, as the first step towards the organization of democracy, that all who add to the wealth of the country shall have a voice in ordering how taxation should be levied and spent. Manhood suffrage could alone supply the power to carry out genuine reform.

But other mere mechanical changes are needed at the same time. That a Parliament should last six years without a dissolution, has been found to be a matter of serious inconvenience to the State at large. Men who know that they are irremovable for so long a period trust to national forgetfulness to cover over their blunders. Many instances could be given of this calculation, and its effects upon the course of public business. Triennial Parliaments, or, better still, a retirement of one-third of the members each year, would keep the House of Commons thoroughly in harmony with the constituencies, and quicken the general interest in political affairs. Equal electoral districts necessarily follow upon manhood or adult suffrage. Any other arrangement would inevitably bring about in a new form that injustice which we wish to get rid of. The right of all to a vote once conceded, no man can claim a greater share in representation than another.

In the same way payment of all election expenses, whether parliamentary or municipal, out of the public funds, is essential. Wealth has already far too much influence, without making political life almost impossible to the poor man, and especially to the working class. Why should a man be called upon to pay a vast fine in order to fill a public office for which his countrymen think him qualified? The working class can never hope to be fairly represented till this has been carried at the least. In the same way, payment of members is but justice. Unpaid work as a whole is bad work, done as a rule for social aggrandizement, personal advancement, or the like. A representative ought to feel that he is the servant of the State, quite open to form his own judgment, but still as much a part of the general executive as any Minister. Moreover, this mere money business must act as a drawback, or almost to the exclusion, of poor men. Few can afford to throw their whole time into the House of Commons work, on Committees, &c., without remuneration. Those who do, have generally contrived as a body – landlords, capitalists, railway directors, &c. – to reimburse themselves in some way at the expense of the country at large.

These four points therefore are imperatively needed as the means towards a better organization:–

- Manhood Suffrage.
- Triennial Parliaments.
- Equal Electoral Districts.
- Payment of Members and especially all Election Expenses, out of public funds.

They are but means to an end; yet it is humiliating to remember that they were demanded in 1848 by a powerful organization, and now here we are in 1881 still without them. Englishmen have lost pluck under middle-class rule. The influence of the perpetual money-getting seems to have exercised a weakening effect on every portion of the body politic. Nowadays, any sturdy demand for plain rights is styled revolutionary; and a sort of cant patter-song of moderation is chanted by both parties, who on all these matters are practically at one. It does one good at such times to breathe the free bluff air of downright agitation, when men call a spade a spade, and a trimmer a useless flabby creature, to be thrown into the political gutter as soon as may be.

For the definite issue we are now debating has been led up to for at least three generations. The shock of the Revolution in France enabled the upper and middle classes here to set back reforms till our day, which were recognized as essential in a far different state of things by such a man as Lord Chatham. Now we see on every side nations beginning to govern themselves wholly for the sake of the people. That government of the people by the people of which noble Abraham Lincoln spoke on the battle-field of Gettysburg as the cause for which men fell there, is the cause which we have yet to fight out peacefully here.

For at this present moment, whilst we are discussing the expediency of this or that step, a process of centralization and decentralization is going forward, which, unless we take means to understand and take advantage of it, will land us all in administrative anarchy. Universal suffrage, giving vent to direct personal interest, but harmonized and consolidated into a general effect for the public good, must be the basis of that new social and political period on which we are now entering. By itself it can do nothing; but it is surely possible, at our stage of political development, to combine the full satisfaction of the wishes of the people, and the improvement of their social position, with the ideal of a great country leading European development by virtue of true sagacity and vigour. It is such an ideal of public advantage that can alone stimulate men to sacrifice their individual crotchets to attain a great end.

To stand still is out of the question. Parliament, as every one can see, no longer holds the position in public esteem, or is able to carry on its work, as it did. How far the House of Lords and the House of Commons may require remodelling is a point on which men differ. That great changes are needed, all are agreed. The House of Lords stands only by reason of its past. Many hesitate to attack it, as the City hesitated to remove Temple Bar. It is antiquated and cumbrous, and unquestionably blocks the way; but there are still historical associations which induce men to shrink from a definite agitation for its overthrow.

Besides, it is at the present time the best debating club of its kind in Europe. There, on great occasions, the traditions of oratory, which are beginning to fade from the House of Commons, may still be found as a living force. But it is sad to see so much ability fired into the air. Their lordships only exchange their ordinary attitude of well-bred indifference and drowsiness for a more active interest when some reactionary motion has to be affirmed to no purpose. Young men who grow up in that dull atmosphere early acquire an apparent consciousness of their own uselessness. Why should they longer suffer, poor fellows, from this hereditary boredom? It would be charitable to relieve them from so false a position as that which they now hold. A closer contact with the moving forces of English political life might perhaps develop in some of them a worthy ambition to lead, instead of languidly attempting to dam back, the current of their time. This at any rate is certain, that the time is rapidly passing away when a caucus of territorial magnates can play at being superior creatures to their fellow-countrymen, and amuse themselves by retarding legislation which the mass of Englishmen have decided upon.

To sweep away any institution altogether is, however, scarcely our English way. So long as it can be advantageously modified we cling to the old form. That the hereditary principle must be done away with as an anachronism and an absurdity would be admitted by thousands, who would still wish to have a second chamber – not to interfere with or hamper the direct representatives of democracy, but to maintain a continuity in general policy which such a body as a reformed House of Commons could scarcely command. Here, of course, is the great difficulty of our party system of Government, and it can never be lessened save by the formation of some great consultative assembly, in which representatives of all portions of our great commonwealth and dependencies find a seat. It may be that the American Senate, devised by men who had thoroughly studied the dangers of waves of popular excitement, is too powerful a body for us to wish to constitute a similar check upon the Lower House; for the Senate in the United States, owing to its method of election, the personal reputation of its members, and the authority accorded, is the powerful House, and with us, if parliamentary government is maintained in its present shape, the House of Commons can scarcely fail to be supreme. The danger of deadlocks with us, however, would not be nearly so great as in our colonies, where the power of the purse is divided.

What we need in place of the House of Lords is a Great Council for the public discussion and revision of treaties, the maintenance of a constant survey of our foreign relations – which will be greatly facilitated when the present system of secret diplomacy is put an end to – and a regulation of the policy towards our great colonies and dependencies, in conjunction with direct representatives from them. These duties are now not performed at all; and during the last twenty years we have had but too many occasions to lament that lack of continuity in our policy which at times makes us the laughing-stock of the world. Such a great consultative and deliberative council might worthily take the place which the House of Lords held when it was really a power in the State. Now it is merely a nuisance; and the sooner a change is made which shall bring the second chamber once more into a useful sphere of existence, the better for the stability of the Constitution in its best sense. Such a modification would indeed, though radical to start, be highly conservative in the best sense in the long-run. The abler men would probably welcome a change which whilst, as we see in France, it makes no great difference in their social distinction – for certain classes cling to lineage as something to worship – freed their hands and enabled them to enter into the real political strife of the day without restraint.

The future of the House of Commons is a very different matter. At the present time, partly by its own fault, and partly by the force of circumstances, that noble historical assembly has also lost influence with the people, because it has grasped at more power than it can conveniently handle, and is far too slow to suggest any reform of itself. Did any body of men, by the way, ever reform themselves? That is really the difficulty we are at present in. There is no power outside the House of Commons to reform the House of Commons; and to hear some members talk, one might suppose it was still the collective wisdom of the nation. Such scenes, however, as those which occurred with regard to the Irish members, the voting on the Bradlaugh oath, and the hopeless block of legislation – occasioned not so much by obstruction, though there has been a great deal of that without the justification which the Irish members could claim on the Coercion Bill, as by the endless flood of conversational small talk which men of no special knowledge or ability seem to think they owe to their constituencies – have gradually convinced the country that a complete change in the functions of Parliament can alone right the existing state of things.

Neither manhood suffrage nor the reform of methods of election will put an end to obstruction, check silly garrulity, or remove the excessive business with which the House of Commons is cumbered. And here we come to a point at which much difference of opinion must necessarily arise. That greater powers should be given to local assemblies to deal with many matters which now come before the House of Commons, may be admitted without dispute; but how far the authority of these local assemblies should extend is, a matter of difference. Irishmen demand home rule, or even separation; Scotchmen and Welshmen have no such anxiety to obtain parliaments to themselves. But with manhood suffrage in full force, it is clear that the rights of the people will be far more completely protected than they are at present, and that power could be more safely handed over to local authorities. National and federal parliaments can scarcely be organized till there is a demand for them. The Irish do make the demand, and the possibility of meeting it without actual disruption is a pressing question at this moment.

In England, Scotland, and Wales, however, the county, the municipality, the township, are old well-understood divisions, and to them, under one or other of the numerous schemes which have been before the public, might be handed over the jurisdiction in respect of many matters on which the House of Commons has at present to be consulted. Such representations, properly elected to transact the rapidly growing business of the whole population, would take an amount of petty work off parliament, with which it ought never to have been saddled. All this, of course, will shortly be attempted; and with the power of the democracy brought to bear for the collective advantage, the old local bodies will be invigorated with fresh life. County assemblies and municipal boards will then perhaps cease to be, as they so often are now, mere inefficient and corrupt vestries. It is unreasonable that the House of Commons should undertake to settle what these local bodies could equally well arrange for themselves. A wide scheme of decentralization, carried out with a view to interesting the whole population in their local business, would but serve to strengthen the House of Commons for dealing with affairs now pushed aside by less important matters to the injury of the whole community, and raise again the character of its debates.

It is remarkable, indeed, that as wealth, power, and political influence have been concentrated in the hands of the upper and middle classes local vigour has to a certain extent died down. In the future the municipality, as we can already see, will have far wider duties to undertake than those which they perform at present. Gas, water, artisans' dwellings – these, instead of being left to individual companies will be undertaken by the local bodies, as also the providing of parks and recreation-grounds. When full power is vested in such corporations and county boards to take what land is needed at a valuation for the purpose of either building or permanent leases for agricultural purposes, a far greater amount of interest will attach to the improvement of the management, and men of a superior character will be anxious to take part in the business. All such decentralization, in the sense that these bodies are given great powers without applying to Parliament, will also act in the direction of peaceful development, and give the working classes that impetus towards social improvement by their own energy which is so manifestly necessary.

At the same time, though municipal and local business may form a good training for local administration, it by no means follows that a good vestryman or alderman makes a good member of Parliament when obligations beyond the range of a three months' bill are under discussion. It is remarkable indeed that in such matters working men, who literally do not know whether their present week's wage will be continued the next, have a far wider idea of their duties, and take a much higher view of the position which a great country like ours ought to assume in its dealings with its dependencies and foreign powers, than mere mercantile men. The latter are far too apt to consider everything from the immediate pounds, shillings, and pence standard. Will such a policy increase immediately the national turn over? then it is excellent. Will it involve doubtful expenditure for a great moral principle, or serious political agitation for a great future national benefit? such a proposal must of necessity be unsound. This sort of reasoning is well enough up to a certain point, and the kind of intelligence which develops it – Lord Derby probably has that sort of capacity to the highest degree of any man living – is most careful to secure economy in local affairs; but where business of national or imperial importance is involved, such counsellors are feeble and dangerous.

Now as in the management of general municipal

improvements and county affairs of all kinds, local energy, and even, in the wide sense, personal objects ought to be allowed fair play, so in these more general concerns, where the necessity for a greater centralization is manifestly increasing, a reformed House of Commons should exercise far more direct control, delegating its authority, as at the present time, to a great officer of State and his department.

All can see quite plainly that in certain matters management by the State is essential to efficiency. It is perhaps a question whether the post and telegraphs ought to be worked at a profit; but no one doubts nowadays that the business is on the whole better and more cheaply done than if it were in private hands. Blunders are made, no doubt; but mistakes are easily complained of and remedied. Obviously the railways must sooner or later follow the same course. This is one of the reasons why local business should be removed from Parliament. It destroys the sense of perspective for members to have constantly to adjudicate on petty private bills, when matters of really great national concern ought to be continually before them. Nothing more shortsighted was ever done by an English Parliament – middle-class business men, too, let us remember – than the turning over of the great new highways of the country to monopolists for ever. This is what has been – nay, what is being, done to the permanent and growing disadvantage of the whole community. No idea seems to have entered the minds of our worthy rulers that this handing over in perpetuity was as mischievous a piece of folly as ever was perpetrated.

We Englishmen often jeer at Frenchmen for their fondness for paternal rule; and we certainly should not submit for a week to many of the restrictions on individual liberty which Republican France bears without a murmur. Their tariff also we regard as injurious, and many of their arrangements mistaken. Yet they were shrewd enough to see that to saddle coming generations with payments to private investors was a grave injury to the nation and a sacrifice of public property. As a result, within fifty or sixty years France will be relieved entirely of her national debt by the falling in of the railways, or transport at cost will be secured to the community. Now that is business; that is foresight for a people. Such an advantage we cannot secure, save by some great change in the right of inheritance or by purchase. The present system cannot be allowed to go on for ever. That the labour of succeeding generations should be eternally handicapped by payments to the labour of the dead, is too preposterous. If turnpikes have been found to be an intolerable nuisance, and fees for bridges have been done away, it is scarcely probable that we shall much longer put up with a system of railway management so entirely opposed to the interests of the mass of the people, as well as of the trading class, as that which now we suffer from. We are a long-suffering people, but we shall never stand that.

This question of monopolies is rapidly coming to the front. The old notion that competition would always come in to serve the community, has proved wholly fallacious. Combination has in many instances, perhaps in most, defeated the calculations of the legislature; and the power of the great companies to fight off those whom they consider intruders, has been exercised without any scruple whatever. All the recent evidence tends in the same direction. The railway companies treat their customers as if the public had been specially created by some beneficent providence for these monopolists to prey upon and get interest for shareholders. This view is natural enough; and we see in America that the system is carried yet further. Monopolies granted by the State are made the means of fleecing the community. Thus once more we have the illusory freedom of contract. The House of Commons, as representative of the people, allows a monopoly to be created, and then this monopoly is used to the public detriment. Unfortunately, the remedy is not so easy as might appear.

The total price of the railways at present quotations would exceed £1,000,000,000, and he would be a bold financier who should propose to increase the national debt by that sum at the present time. But private interests cannot be allowed to stand permanently in the way of the community at large. The right of interference has never been disputed. If the House of Commons had not been full of representatives of the Railway interest, steps would long since have been taken by the Government to secure for Englishmen at large far greater advantage in return for the monopoly granted. It is plain, for example, that the State could construct a railroad from London say to Liverpool or Manchester, at a very much less cost than the capitalized value of either of the existing lines. If the stockholders have not taken this fact into account, that is their own look-out. No Parliament nor any succession of Parliaments, could guarantee a monopoly against another company that showed good cause for the construction of a line, still less could it be assured against the State. Consequently when it becomes necessary, as it shortly must, to acquire the railways, no such absurd estimate of value need be made as in the case of the London water companies. Our tendency has been for the nation to show itself too considerate of so-called vested interests, simply because the classes which hold those vested interests have had the entire control in every way – to assume, indeed, when the State has to deal with them that some exceptional price must be paid. This is quite incorrect. When the decision is come to that for the national interest the railways should be acquired, it would be perfectly fair to purchase at a valuation, without any reference to a future monopoly-value, which does not and could not exist against the country at large. A special issue of terminable annuities might be made to cover the whole matter. But without entering on details, it is clear that such a notification as that lately issued with reference to workmen's trains by the Metropolitan Railways will probably bring this whole question to a climax. [1]

That State management would pay, there is very little doubt. Improved organization would produce a profit by the reduction of working expenses. But far more important than any idea of profit, is the prospect, under proper direction, of cheapening transport, and securing for the working-classes really cheap travel in the neighbourhood of large cities. It is scarcely too much to say that sixpenny weekly tickets, available for any distance within ten miles, coupled with a well-regulated system of artisans' dwellings, erected by the muncipality and let at rents to cover cost of construction, would completely change the whole life of great cities, reducing rents for unwholesome tenements, and gradually leading to a better condition in every respect. It is also by no means certain that the suggestion made by a Civil Engineer that a one shilling fare should apply to the whole United Kingdom, would not, in some modified form, prove as great a success as the penny post. In any case it is manifest that the Railways are the national highways, that in regard to the transfer of both goods and passengers they work for the shareholders and not for the community, and that consequently the business of the country is carried on at a growing disadvantage. Besides, the land and the railways are inseparably bound up together, and those who talk about dealing freely with the one without touching the other, overlook a most important feature in the whole business.

The chief objection to the acquirement of the railways even on terms which might seem highly advantageous from a financial point of view, would doubtless be the danger of increasing the power of the Government by the formation of so vast a bureaucracy. But this ought to involve no political danger, with full publicity and a distinct removal of the railways from the sphere of State patronage. Certainly the fear of what might happen in this way ought not to keep back the country from laying hands upon a set of corporations whose directors work their influence with the most perfect selfishness, using their railroads to help their politics, and their politics to help their railroads. That sort of see-saw is quite as objectionable as any bureaucratic taint. With the advance of democracy, and the reference of all questions to the people, it has become more and more clear that the Civil Service, as a profession, should be kept clear of politics and party. Where this is not done all sorts of mischief creep in; where it is, and full publicity is maintained – an essential point too – there the organization is a great gain to all. The right of representation of grievances by State officials must of course be fully secured.

Railways, then, like the control of mines, factories, and workshops, must be placed under the State – the former for management, the latter for supervision. These are matters which affect the entire national welfare, and can only be adequately dealt with by national ordinance. Manifestly rivers, canals, and drainage, fall under the same head. The neglect of these as a matter of national importance is really most astonishing. At present our rivers – the watershed and drinking source of the whole country – are treated as municipalities, or even as individuals, think fit. This too, though the urban population, as the late census clearly shows, is increasing in density almost to the danger-point. Decentralization in this matter is really ruinous to the public interest. Drainage works are carried out, sewage and refuse of the most unpleasant nature is disposed of, without much reference to the effect which the action of one town or one owner may produce in other directions. No doubt there are bye-laws and statutes, but they have never been properly put in force. The injury already done by this separatist system is enormous. For the future all arrangements affecting rivers or canals should be under the management of a public department, specially constituted to take in the bearings of the whole subject, whilst leaving to the county assemblies, local boards, municipalities, and even township vestries, the fullest powers of carrying out their own projects within the limits that concern only themselves.

As the powers of these local bodies to acquire land and other property can scarcely fail to be largely increased in the near future and their rights to make improvements extended, it is the more essential that to start with the due position of the central authority should be clearly defined, secured, and strengthened. Of the existing departments, or the proposal to create a Minister of Agriculture and Commerce, it is needless to speak here; that is a mere matter of convenience in separating functions now combined. But in all such matters the tendency towards the simultaneous operation of causes which tend to centralization, as well as those which invite the strengthening of local forces, ought not to be neglected. To create social or political machinery is beyond the power of assemblies or autocrats; to take care that the natural growth of a nation should be fostered instead of hindered is the true function of a statesman. Surely it is reasonable to foresee that the existing fierce competition will in many directions besides that of railroads develop into combination,and thus gradually be turned to the advantage of all.

There is no need to fear the crushing of individuality in all this. Rather will there gradually rise up a higher individuality, when each man can look to his own development as contributing to the advancement of all. But the success of any movement depends upon the mass of the people, and the readiness of men who ought already to have voting power to press forward earnestly the interests of themselves and their children. Nothing can be done unless the people are prepared to organize their forces. Here, however, are what seem the natural reforms demanded for the organization of the great democracy on which the future of England depends:–

- Manhood suffrage, with the other electoral reforms already specified.
- The reform of the House of Lords into a Great Council, in which our colonies and dependencies should

be fully represented.

• The restriction of the House of Commons as a whole to dealing with national questions; the arrangement of great committees, &c., being adjusted to the changed conditions

• A great increase of power to be given to county boards and municipal councils, to purchase land for public use, &c., so that even without federal parliaments all matters affecting separate districts could be dealt with locally, subject to the general law.

• The entire system of national railways to be purchased at a valuation, by annuities secured on the railways, and managed by a State department in the interest of the mass of the community.

• A department to be formed dealing more directly with the main watercourses, canals, and forestry than any now in existence.

• An extension of the Factory and Mines Acts, and inspection of shipping, so as to constitute the State more completely the protector of men and women who under freedom of contract are bound to risk their lives and their health.

To these may be added the social reforms previously advocated:–

• Free compulsory education for all.
• Fight hours to be the working day.
• Compulsory erection of artisans' dwellings by municipalities and county assemblies in place of unhealthy houses or dwellings removed for improvements.
• Cheap trains, at the rate of sixpence for a weekly ticket, on all lines within ten miles of a great city.

By these means centralization and decentralization

would have free play to work themselves out; a great pressure would be removed from our historical assemblies – both of which would be strengthened by a reduction of numbers and a more direct representation of the mass of the people and the interests of the whole empire.

Those who suppose that democracy tends to disorganization and anarchy quite misread the signs of the times. Wherever educated democracy has the freest play, precisely there will be found the most complete organization, both in public and in private affairs. The danger arises, if at all, from the opposite quarter. But Englishmen have clearly begun to see that in this direction only can their further development go on. The aristocracy had their day; and in 1832 their power was shaken, to be gradually sapped up to the present time. They have chosen to throw in their lot with the bourgeoisie, and to trade on the necessities of the labourer with them. For fifty years we have experienced middle-class rule: that now is tottering to its fall, with no record but selfishness in home affairs. Now comes the turn of England at large as represented by the men who are really the England of to-day. It is for them to see that their future is worthy of the greatness of their country, ensuring the physical and moral welfare of all by organization and self-sacrifice.

Notes

1. The infamous overwork of their servants by the Railway Companies as recently exposed, is alone enough to call for immediate State interference. The brutal greed of corporations was never exhibited in a more shameless form at the expense of both the men and the public.

Chapter V Ireland

It is perhaps the most telling commentary upon our government of Ireland, that in dealing with the affairs of that island English statesmen are still obliged to proceed in every respect upon the separate system. Ireland has been an integral portion of the United Kingdom for eighty years, and yet we have at this time more than 30,000 troops and 12,000 constabulary occupied in keeping down a serious rebellion. This, at any rate, is the contention of the people immediately responsible for that law and order to secure which a liberal ministry has been content to override the first guarantee of all liberty, and to proclaim the capital of the country in a state of siege. There is, perhaps, no need for the mass of Englishmen to take special blame to themselves for the harm which has been done. They are scarcely responsible for a policy over which as a mass they have exercised no real control. Yet it is impossible to compare what has happened with Ireland to that which has taken place in regard to Alsace and Lorraine, or Savoy and Nice, without being compelled to acknowledge that in all that relates to a subject people they manage these matters better in France. Reforms in Ireland – political, religious, economical, social – have in every case been delayed, until they have ceased to be boons to the people; pressure from without has been waited for in every instance, until it took an explosive shape; and men who to start with were ready to welcome moderate measures, have been driven to combine on an almost revolutionary programme, from sheer hopelessness of obtaining justice in any other way.

There is no need to go back to the history of centuries of misgovernment to account for what we see to-day. Doubtless the wrongs of the past have done much to embitter the relations between two countries which ought to be at one; but enough has occurred within the lifetime of the present generation to account for that sad state of affairs which politicians of all parties deplore and all ought to strive to remedy. In Ireland, as in England and Scotland, the people have been deprived of the possession of their own land in favour of a small minority. Such manufactures as existed having been destroyed long since by English legislation, and Ireland not producing iron and coal to a profitable extent, the men have been unable to seek in the cities the work which their brothers in destitution across the channel were enabled to obtain. Hence arose that earth-hunger which enabled landowners to exact rack-rents, and left the people to multiply on poor food, nearer and ever nearer to the limit of starvation. Foreign conquest and absenteeism have aggravated the mischief politically and economically. Difference of race and religion rendered grave social ills more difficult to deal with. But the great catastrophe of 1847 ought to have opened our eyes to some portion of the truth – ought to have shown the people of England that here we had an exceptional problem to deal with, and that such dominance as had been established was discreditable to the rulers and ruinous to the ruled.

That fearful famine formed the starting-point of the modern history of Ireland. It had been predicted by men of very different views and capacities. It came, as such cataclysms sometimes do, in its worst possible shape, and was followed up by a revolutionary legislation which all can now see was most unfortunate. Instead of accepting the wise recommendations of the Devon Commission – made, be it remembered, three years before the famine – or the still wiser advice of Lord Beaconsfield, given about the same time, but later so unfortunately withdrawn – full rights were given to landlords, new and old, to uproot the population, tear down their miserable dwellings, and hurry them across the Atlantic, famine fever wearing out their bodies, and fury at such injustice and tyranny rankling in their minds. Who that has read through the details of that miserable time, when men, women, and children were turned out of their holdings, – as they are now being turned out, though happily in far fewer numbers – to wander in starvation and misery along the highways, can wonder that a generation has grown up in Ireland and in the United States which regards with positive hatred England and all that belongs to her? The very Encumbered Estates Act, a most valuable measure in itself if carefully carried out, forced the lands of ancient proprietors who understood the people, not into the control of the State, which would have acted with some consideration, but into the hands of foreign speculators, who bought at a low price with the express purpose of raising the rents upon the tenants. An absenteeism was thus created worse than that which had existed before. In the end, doubtless, good came out of evil for those who were left; but twenty-four years elapsed before any effort was made on the part of the Imperial Parliament to secure to the mass of the people of Ireland some portion of the benefits which even the Devon Commission had urged.

All this while, over the greater part of Ireland a purely agricultural community had no security of tenure of any sort or kind, and the church of the small minority was kept up at the expense of those who were of a different creed. Irishmen, who in the United States did an amount of hard work which almost reconciled the not very sympathetic Americans to their gregarious habits in the cities, and their religious belief, so hostile to the Puritanism which even sceptics in that great country still consider it prudent to affect – Irishmen, who in our colonies, notwithstanding many defects, have brought themselves to the front by their industry, were accused in their own country of idleness and indifference, because, after centuries of misrule, they could see no object in giving their masters their labour for nothing. That was really the fact. All accounts agree that wherever in Ireland a man has a permanent tenure of a fair piece of land, in the great majority of cases he works as hard as an Indian *ryot* or French peasant-proprietor. It is absurd, of course, to deny the influence of race and climate;

none would contend that a Saxon and an Irishman have the same qualities. But the remarkable feature in the whole matter is, that the descendants of Saxons have been just as much opposed, and more violent in showing their opposition to the landlord-made legislation, as the Irish themselves. Nor have they been one whit more industrious than their Celtic neighbours. The descendants of Cromwell's soldiery, though more turbulent under injustice, have not been any more inclined to give the fruits of their labour to their landlords than the Catholics around them. But wherever tenant-right has been introduced and fairly held to, there, notwithstanding the fact that economical disturbances – American competition, slackened demand for store beasts in England and Scotland, no requirement for casual Irish labour in the summer – have affected the whole island, there peace and quiet have in the main prevailed.

As a mere matter of national business it would have been cheap to have given the tenants a permanent hold upon the soil, even if the landlords had been compensated beyond the value of what they parted with. The cost of the maintenance of a large army and a great constabulary in Ireland cannot well be estimated in actual money. Many considerations are involved. But in any case, have we the right to prevent 5,500,000 people from settling their own local business in their own way? Surely there is not an Englishman of either party who does not feel that our present attitude is somewhat hypocritical. It may be that Irishmen if left to themselves would not make the best possible settlement of their own affairs; but are English landlords qualified to judge of the matter for them any better? They have hitherto constituted the ultimate court of appeal. When we speak of the unfairness of Irish juries in agrarian cases, let us at least remember the persistent unfairness of the great English jury of legislators on this question of life or death to the people of Ireland. Even when the House of Commons has been willing to give in, the House of Lords has stood by their own class; and here, in the last quarter of the nineteenth century, we have as honest and patriotic a man as ever lived, hotheaded and furious though he be, taken and put in gaol, though also a member of Parliament, for having denounced, and urged his countrymen to resist, a most tyrannous system of evictions. And let us bear this in mind, that unfortunately the immense majority of the Liberal party have been quite delighted at the arrest of Mr. Dillon, and cheered like madmen at the arrest of Mr. Davitt.

The history of the last few months of panic and misgovernment in Ireland is worth consideration by all who hold that freedom and justice are worth something in themselves, aside from the question whether a party chooses to throw them over or not. What has occurred since July of last year is alone enough to prove conclusively that no country could be peaceable under such a rule as we have inflicted upon the people of Ireland. Steady despotism would be far preferable to such miserable incapacity and vacillation as has been exhibited.

For here is what has taken place. Last year, after Ireland had suffered from a period of severe privation, which fell upon the small tenant-farmers and the labourers with redoubled severity owing to their being unable to obtain work in England, the landlords – or rather a few of the baser sort – began to evict their tenantry. Hunger and sense of injustice combined made men desperate. The Land Bill of 1870, though by no means a satisfactory measure, had given a tenant a certain claim for compensation for disturbance in all cases save non-payment of rent. If evicted for not paying his rent, however, this right to compensation was gone, and he went out upon the high roads a pauper, with the workhouse as his only refuge. This eviction, therefore, was felt to be a greater hardship than any previous eviction, because it was not only harsh, but in the view of the tenant unjust. Good landlords, of course, were considerate in Ireland as elsewhere: people like Lord Lansdowne, whose idea of landed property necessarily involved serfdom and servility (as he was good enough to inform the Americans, of all people in the world, through the **Chicago Tribune**), were naturally eager not to lose the advantage of any misfortune among their tenantry. That few should have acted in this contemptible fashion gives no conception of the alarm produced. Not a very large proportion of tenants in the year are rack-rented; but that proportion acts as a damper upon thousands of others in improving their farms, and prevents them from making the best of their labour.

These evictions, then, having begun, and going on in an increasing ratio, the Government boldly and rightly introduced a Bill of the most carefully-guarded character, to prevent downright oppression and tyranny from being brought to bear. That Bill, after some of the most bitter discussions in the House of Commons and in the press ever known, was passed by a considerable majority, the Prime Minister making himself prominent of course in its championship, and saying, what recent events have proved only too clearly to be the truth, that if it were not passed we should be within a measureable distance of civil war. This, be it remembered, also took place after the Government had declined to renew the Peace Preservation Act, on the express ground that it was contrary to the principles of liberty and Liberalism. Very well. What followed was not only probable but certain. The House of Lords, seeing the whole right of eviction when contrary to common interest jeopardized by the measure, threw out the Bill. The Government – that is the opinion of all parties in Ireland – winked at the agitation which followed. That agitation was, in view of what had passed, justifiable and righteous, and was carried on, when once the Land League had obtained a hold upon the people, with surprisingly little bloodshed or bad action. A vast agrarian strike was organized – not against all rent, but against rent above a certain valuation. There were also rattenings and boycottings, where men took land from which tenants had been evicted.

Many things, no doubt, were done, and are being done now, most obnoxious to Englishmen: the injuries to cattle in particular are dastardly in the extreme. Gradually, as evictions went on, and help was received from sympathizers in America, temper rose, and the feeling – mingled with that race and religious hatred which is the worst feature of all, because the least capable of yielding to reason – became very bitter.

But what has it been after all? A trifle beside the agitations of 1848 and 1833, and to be met – that was the just contention of the Government and the Liberal party – not by repression, but by reform. "Force is no remedy," said Mr. Bright, strong as he always has been on this Irish question; and there was not a genuine liberal Englishman in the country who would not have stood behind those words. And force has been no remedy – has only aggravated the whole mischief. But what comes now? The Cabinet having been summoned in hot haste in December, decided that in these days we must deal with popular grievances, even when exaggerated, by reason and argument, and not by bullets and buckshot – and separated without calling Parliament together. A little while and Mr. Forster again comes over, with woe-begone visage, and Parliament is summoned. A Coercion Act and Arms Act become law, at what a strain to our whole system of parliamentary government we perhaps yet scarcely know. Members of the House of Commons, acting no doubt very provokingly and very foolishly, but still within their rights, are silenced and ejected; and Ireland is put under a suspensive state of siege.

Thus the very Government which had declared that evictions of a certain kind were most unjust, and must be restrained, put in the hands of the landlords as complete a machinery of eviction as they had ever possessed, and backed it up by pouring troops into the country. And evictions soon multiplied. Men, women, and children were turned out under circumstances which reproduced here in England would have brought about an insurrection.

What? Let us for once use plain language about these things. Has a Government, have any number of landlords, sitting in Parliament to represent a dominant caste, the right to turn a man, his wife, and children, out into the bitter air of January, because, poor devil, there had been a famine, and he could not pay his rent? I say No. Last year the vast majority of the House of Commons said No; and if the question were fairly put to them I believe the vast majority of Englishmen to-day would say No. Ireland, it is true, cannot hope to resist successfully such shameful oppression, but why should English working men sanction and support action which, if applied to themselves, they would rise against? The truth is, and this will shortly become apparent to all, the tenant-farmers and labourers of Ireland are fighting the battle of the working-classes of England in relation to the land, and get far less support than they ought to get on grounds where they are both agreed. This, at least, is certain, that unless the Land League had been formed, and the Irish had stood together in a great economical movement, no such Land Bill as that of 1881 would have been brought before the English House of Commons at all. The Land League, whether it be called communistic, nationalistic, or what not, has brought the first genuine attempt yet made at reform within the range of practical politics.

The facts in relation to Irish land have been made known to all by means of the propaganda which they carried on. There are but 12,000 landowners in all Ireland, and 1,000 of them own two-thirds of the island. One fourth of these landowners are permanent absentees, who take their rents to the amount of millions sterling out of the country, and spend them elsewhere. And yet six-sevenths of the population have to derive their subsistence from the land, and naturally enough compete against one another to such an extent as to raise rents to a high figure. Say the theorists, Irishmen are too fond of land, are too much given to agriculture. This is quite absurd. In the United States the Americans make precisely the opposite complaint. They say that the Irish are too much addicted to crowding into the cities; and so they undoubtedly are. But in Ireland they stick to the land, for the best of all possible reasons, that there is nothing else for them to get a living out of; and as arable land is being continually turned into pasture by the large landowners and large farmers, there is less and less employment for them as labourers, and less and less land which they can take up to feed themselves and their families upon. No one disputes the sad condition of a vast proportion of the tenant farmers who hold under fifteen acres, which amount to more than half the whole 500,000. Those who drag out a miserable existence in Mayo and Connemara, would be no better off if they held their patches in fee. Migration and emigration are the only possible remedies for these people.

But here, as in England, the first step is to get the land out of the hands of the large proprietors, and enable the people of Ireland to work out their own social difficulties. The great main drainage works which some reformers clamour for, cannot possibly be carried out for the benefit of the landowners, whose properties would be improved; neither can reclamation go on without some regard to economical and physical conditions. The tendency of bog to revert to bog is as well-known in Scotland as in Ireland. That Ireland is in itself a poor country has lately been disputed, and with good reason. It is not a poor country, but a poor people, that we have to deal with. In Ireland, to take the same comparison as was made in the case of England, the population has decreased nearly 3,000,000 in thirty years, and the assessment to income-tax has grown by £15,000,000 annually. Moreover, the deposits in the banks point in the same direction. Ireland itself, therefore, has become far richer in the last generation, but the distribution of that wealth is so faulty that a year of bad crops means little short of famine to a large population.

Happily, the Bill of 1881 accepts principles which have hitherto been scouted as communistic. The distinct object which underlies the complicated economical clauses is to secure to a portion at least of the population that right to the fruits of their labour, of which they have hithertobeen deprived by landlords under the name of freedom of contract. Why is it that peasant proprietorship has, on the whole, been beneficial where people have been settled on the soil? Surely because in this way alone can a man and his family, in our system of society, be secure of the fruits of his own labour. In every other case, where the poor man wishes to obtain employment he is deprived of a portion of his produce for the benefit of others. Unquestionably the Liberal Government has made a great step forward when it recognizes in a definite measure that freedom of contract, where the force is all on one side, may, and in many cases must mean, injustice and tyranny.

But to suppose that any Land Bill, however carefully drawn – that any courts, however impartial – will settle the Irish question, is to assume far more than the facts warrant. Nothing is more noteworthy than the disposition of the tenant-farmers all over the country to sink their differences in view of the agitation for a mitigated form of the three F's, which will probably break down – or a peasant proprietorship, which will involve the pressure of the *gombeen* man. This latter point is worth a moment's consideration. India is, it is true, different in many ways from Ireland; but there the right of eviction by the moneylender has been found more dangerous and objectionable than eviction by any other method. Should not restriction be placed on mortgage and bill of sale here, too, if we desire to prevent similar expropriations from taking place there, and giving rise to a distinctly socialist agitation, which could not be dealt with under present conditions? But the Land Bill as it stands constitutes such an enormous advance upon what seemed possible even a few months ago, that Irishmen would be foolish indeed not to make as much of it as they can. To secure the tenants in their holdings, to obtain assistance in settling a peasant proprietory on the land, and help for emigration and migration, are steps towards that pacification which full patience alone can bring about. But for the shameful and silly Coercion Bill a hope might have arisen, not of a settlement of all Irish difficulties —such impatience to get rid of the natural troubles of administration argues weakness and incapacity—but of a better understanding between the English and the Irish peoples.

That, little as it may seem to be so at this moment, has really been the outcome of the agitation. For the first time in recent Irish history, a vast number of Englishmen of all classes have felt that wrong was being done in their name when the common rights of the United Kingdom were suspended in deference to the clamour of an interested and panic-stricken minority. Even the race hatred and the jealousy of keen competitors in the labour-market have been to a certain extent laid aside in view of the fact that injustice was being done. Had the Irish managed their own case better, and kept religious differences altogether out of sight when a political end was in view, this understanding between the democracy of the two countries might have already progressed even farther than it has. There need be no real difference. There is room enough and to spare for the workers of both races under a better system than that which has hitherto found favour. We are, let us hope, approaching the time when we shall endeavour to rule in any case with the consent of the majority – when the highest aim of every statesman will be to reconcile all to a beneficial union, in which every member is contented and free.

That many grievances still remain unredressed even if the Land Bill is passed with reasonable amendment, is unfortunately but too certain. That absurd playing at Viceroyalty in Dublin, with an English Chief Secretary, and a worn-out bureaucracy at the Castle, would aggravate a less touchy people than the Irish. What do they want with a Viceroy and underlings, any more than the Scotch? Why should Irishmen more than Scotchmen be shut out from the management of their own affairs? "They hate you, it is said, and long to drive you out." Has any reason for love been given? At least let us wait to see whether a definite alliance between the English and Irish democracies be not possible, before continuing to support such methods as have hitherto been favoured. Local administration there must be. The management of local business in Ireland as a whole must henceforth be carried on by Irishmen, if there is to be any success at all. That process of decentralization which must go on in Scotland, Wales, and England, is applicable to Ireland too. There, more than here even, the railway, and drainage, and road systems need to be under one great administration. Let them in Heaven's name try their hand with manhood suffrage, at the improvement of their own country; leave them the task of carrying out the detail of the reforms they have rightly forced us to adopt.

This at least we must all admit, that we cannot; continue parliamentary government if we are persistently to run counter to the opinions of the majority of 5,000,000 of people represented in our own House of Commons. It is because separation would be injurious to both countries, as mutual understanding would be beneficial, that Irishmen should at length be granted fair play. Take the absentees, for instance. They are not dealt with; and yet no man can hold that absenteeism is not a serious drawback to Irish prosperity. Such a question concerns the whole country most seriously; but their compulsory expropriation or a heavy exceptional taxation – which commended itself even to Lord George Bentinck – has not been suggested by the Government. The labourers also have to be considered. It is true that the fullest justice to the farmers does not directly benefit them, though the well-being of one class might slowly re-act upon the other. Here again is encountered, in a less complicated shape, the same problem that is met with in England – how to benefit the real workers on the soil at the same time that the most is made of the land. The 500,000 tenant farmers of Ireland form, however, a very different proportion of the entire population, as well as of the agricultural population, from that which a similar class does here with us. To improve their condition without injustice to others, if this can be done, is already much gained.

There is no reason however, why we should stop there. Men who know that they are secure of possession are always ready to reclaim land, and might well be given the option of taking part in such reclamation, or in being assisted to obtain farms in English colonies. Let us not, however, lose sight of the principles involved in all such proposals. We recognize thereby that the State is responsible for the removal of the causes which can be proved to lead to the wretched poverty of the mass of the people. We are entering plainly upon the path of restriction of selfish competition, because, under certain conditions it has failed in agriculture as it has in other directions. Hitherto in Ireland brute force – the brute force of the people of England – has stood behind the dominant class, ready to maintain their views of a political economy which might have been invented in the interest of monopolists. A peaceful revolution has to be brought about, and the first step has been taken. Those, however, who contend that the modification of the land laws of Ireland must extend to England have right on their side. It is impossible any longer to use two sets of arguments on the two sides of the Irish Channel. When, therefore, fixity of tenure, purchase of property, reclamation of land, assisted emigration, and main drainage, are accepted for Ireland, we are not far – we could not be far – from the consideration of similar proposals in England and Scotland.

But even supposing the land question in a fair way of settlement, and local administration set on foot, there remain the race and religious hatreds to consider. These of course are difficulties of a very different character from any which Acts of Parliament can touch. How can Celts and Saxons, Catholics and Protestants, live together in unity? Yet such things have been; and at this moment the leader of the irreconcilable Irish party is neither an Irishman nor a Catholic. Leave the Irish more liberty to arrange their own business, and they will find out some way of getting on with one another, when once the injustice complained of for centuries has been remedied. Ireland has been conquered by arms from generation to generation; it remains for us to conquer finally by justice, magnanimity and consideration.

Many of the noblest names in English history and literature are those of Irishmen; the Irish party in the House of Commons to-day contains men of ability out of all proportion to its numbers; the two most distinguished of our younger generals are Irishmen by birth. Would it not be well, then, for all to consider whether, even at the cost of some sacrifice of consistency, and some forgetfulness of past domination, the loyalty of such a people could be secured, by a freedom which is yet reconcilable with common action? The national feeling now running so high in Ireland could find as full an outlet in the British Empire as that of Scotland, when once it is understood that supremacy is no longer claimed in the interests of a small minority, but to give satisfaction to the high ideals of empire and greatness which a petty island like Ireland, overshadowed perpetually by English power, could never attain. A complete agreement between England and Ireland will be possible only when the people of both countries can control their own policy, and secure at home and abroad that the benefit of the many, not the gain of the few, should be the end.

Chapter VI India

If Ireland, a little island close to our own shores, its people speaking our language, sharing our civilization and religion, with all its problems lying, as it were, in the hollow of our hand and open to inspection with the naked eye – if, after centuries of absolute rule over the inhabitants, we are beginning to confess that the matter is well-nigh too hard for us, and look to enlisting Irishmen in the government of their own country as our only hope of success in the future – if, I say, this little business has plagued us so sore, what are we to think of the task of ruling 200,000,000 of people, of totally different race, language, civilization, and creeds, thousands of miles away from England, by means of 900 young gentlemen who do not set foot in the country till they are over twenty years of age, and work without the slightest help from the natives in the higher branches of administration? Yet this is what we, the English people, are now trying to do in India; and with such unfortunate results to the inhabitants, that it is absolutely essential that the great mass of the community, on whose shoulders now rests the weight of this vast empire, should take the matter into their own hands. This, indeed, is now the only hope that the English people will see the mischief that is being done, and insist that neither vested interests nor regard for individual reputations shall longer stand in the way of absolutely essential reforms.

No man can read the history of our early conquests in India without a strange admixture of feeling. Deeds of the noblest heroism and determination are found side by side with the records of such meanness, cruelty, and greed, that at times we doubt whether it is possible that qualities so different should have belonged to the same race. A mere merchant company, humbly suing for permission to trade, grew into power and influence in spite of themselves, till they became of necessity the heirs of the Great Mogul, and the conquerors of the rising Mahratta confederation; their clerks and supercargoes, their shopmen and peddlers, figured forth before the world as warriors, statesmen, and administrators. Whilst the king and the aristocracy were losing, by sheer ignorance and incompetence, the noblest inheritance across the Atlantic that ever fell to the lot of any nation, ordinary Englishmen were conquering an empire just in the way of everyday business, which, had it been properly managed, would in some degree have compensated for that monstrous blunder. A great and ancient civilization had fallen under their control, and it needed but a right comprehension of its tendencies to lead the people on, with little of change, to a wider and a higher development, which should have been to the advantage of all. This was the idea of some of the nobler spirits, who saw clearly that a growth of thousands of years could not suddenly be twisted in accordance with foreign notions without grave danger of injury to rulers and ruled. To raise the tone of the native Governments to the best native standard, slowly introducing the leaven of Western ideas into the administration without altering the form of society or pursuing the fatal policy of complete annexation – this was the view of men who had, unfortunately, too little weight as against more vehement counsellors.

The East India Company itself, however, protested constantly against the violent methods of its own servants; but the inexorable necessity of paying interest had, very early in its history, a most baneful influence upon the system pursued by us in India. Annexation became the rule; and even forty or fifty years ago the natives of India had begun to discuss the effect of the drain of produce to England consequent upon the multitudes of fortunes made by Englishmen and withdrawn on their leaving. The nabobs who returned after shaking the pagoda-tree, represented so much wealth taken out of India, which was never returned. Nevertheless, the rule of the East India Company was on the whole economical. It was soon found out that countries governed by foreigners, in which the old native system had been broken down, seemed somehow not to have the elasticity and power of recovery for which India had been celebrated for centuries. India, the administrators in Leadenhall Street discovered was a poor country, not to be treated as if untold wealth could be taken for the asking without harming the people.

To enter upon the beneficial changes made in native usages, the noble work of Sleeman in uprooting the Thugs, of Outram in settling the Bheels, of Edwardes on the Indus border, or, on a wider field, the reforms adopted by Lord William Bentinck, would be to extend this chapter far beyond the limits of this little work. Natives of India know well that had Englishmen confined their efforts to such objects as these nothing but good would have come of their rule. To this day the government of the old East India Company, in those countries where good native customs were respected and the people not worried, is looked back to with regard and even affection. Men who went out to India as mere boys got to know the people, and loved them; they made their homes in the country, and returning but rarely to England, held a very different position from that of their successors of to-day.

Asia is the land of long memories, and those who treat its people with justice, firmness, and consideration pass on their legacy of good feeling to the next generation. All who read the writings of Metcalfe, Shore, Malcolm, Mountstuart Elphinstone, Henry Lawrence, Meadows Taylor, or Sleeman, will find that below the surface there is a constant undercurrent of regret at the needless Europeanization which they see going on. And the natives of India have ever been most easily led by men who, whilst combatting their faults, were not above appreciating their good qualities, even when they have shown themselves rigorous and exacting. Thus it happened that, notwithstanding many great errors, and a gradual impoverishment, which was then scarcely perceived, the agricultural population of British India – fully three-fourths of that vast population – was loyal to the rule of the great Company when Lord Dalhousie was appointed Governor-General. It was the mission of this arbitrary bigot to overthrow all the best traditions of our rule in India, to shock every native idea of justice or good faith, to commence that course of unscrupulous annexation and wholesale Europeanization from which our Empire is now suffering, and to lead up by his policy to one of the most serious rebellions that ever shook the power of any Government. The great Mutiny of 1857 was the direct outcome of Lord Dalhousie's headlong career of violence and chicanery. How the rebellion was put down, and what marvellous vigour and tenacity our countrymen showed in resisting the attack of their own trained soldiery, assisted in the more recently annexed territory by the people themselves, are matters of history. It was again a story of marvellous capacity chequered by grave mistakes.

Peace was at length restored; the rule of the East India Company came to an end; and with the assumption of the government by the Crown the English people became directly responsible for the beneficent management of their own great dependency. Throughout the fierce conflict which was waged the sympathy of the mass of the people was with us rather than with the mutineers. If it had not been, we could not possibly have overcome the rebellion. Here, then, if ever in history, was an opportunity for the governing race. It lay with Englishmen to accept the better portion of the system which had been superseded, and to retain the goodwill of the people by light taxation and consideration of their ancient customs.

Unfortunately a different course was adopted. At first all went well. Lord Canning, to his eternal honour, kept his head in panic-stricken Calcutta, and refused to allow millions to be treated with cruelty and injustice because a few infamous ruffians had been guilty of horrible, never-to-be-forgotten outrages. The Queen's Proclamation of 1858 was an admirable document, rightly called the Great Charter of India. Princes and people looked forward to period when all the advantages which had been secured to them by the Company – peace, order, freedom from exaction – should be combined with a gradual preparation for self-government and a careful reorganization of native rule under English guidance. But it was not to be. The word went forth from high quarters that India had been neglected, that what she stood in need of was English capital, at five per cent. guaranteed interest paid half-yearly – and English energy, at very high salaries paid quarterly. India, in fact, became the outlet for the savings of the upper and middle classes and an opening for their sons. Now began the reign of capital in good earliest and with it a pressure of taxation, an increase of famines, a deterioration of the soil, and an impoverishment of the mass of the people unprecedented in the long history of India.

But the administration comes first. In this, one fatal principle has been followed out for the last three-and-twenty years. Wherever room could be found for a European, he has been chosen in place of a native. Even in the judicial department, where the natives have greatly distinguished themselves, none of the highly-paid posts are open to them – although at a lower salary, and with less important positions, they try cases involving quite as grave issues as those tried by the Europeans. The extent to which this employment of Europeans has been carried in every department, surpasses belief. Young natives are educated in the colleges for the highest class of administrative work, but no prizes are ever open to them. They receive the compliments of the Chancellor of the University, who is perhaps also the Governor of the Presidency, on their ability – and then they find themselves ousted by a number of Englishmen from posts in which they might fairly hope to serve their country.

Now this has been very far worse under the Crown than it ever was in the Company's time. In the Public Works Department alone, the European establishment actually cost £2,300,000, a year or two ago; this too, though the natives of India are specially apt at engineering, and all the great irrigation works in the country of any real value have been built by natives, or constructed by Europeans on native principles. Where these have been abandoned the grossest blunders have been made, and millions of acres of land ruined. Time after time requests have been put forward by the people of India, through the only channel open to them, that the total amount paid in salaries to Europeans in India should be published, but this has never been done. The effect of this excessive employment of Englishmen is most serious in every way. Millions sterling every year which might go to the people of the country are taken by foreigners, who, though honest enough, and in some respects more capable than natives, yet really devour the substance of the people whose country they no doubt wish to benefit. More than this, in addition to the salaries they receive in the country, and spend on luxuries which a native would rarely dream of, or the savings which they bear away to England when they depart, every European who leaves Government employment receives a pension, which likewise is so much paid by India to Englishmen out of the country. But there is a further objection still. By this enormous mass of super-incumbent Europeans, who fill every office of importance in a country inhabited by 200,000,000 people, those who might be in training for self-government, and who in time might be able to carry on our best methods without their drawbacks, are turned into a disaffected class. These men see their country, as they think, ruined in the interest of foreigners who have less and less sympathy with the people they rule.

Europeanization is stunting all natural growth in India, and this with less and less excuse every day; for civilians and others no longer live in India as they used to do, rarely make real friends of the people, and are perpetually moved about from post to post or come home on furlough. But they equally prevent any change of system; and on their return to England they form, with some few noble exceptions, a compact body, opposed both by interest and tradition to any real justice to India.

Now if this administration were on the whole successful, it would not even then outweigh the enormous economical drawbacks involved. As, however, it is a failure in almost every branch, and we are now obliged to go back in sheer desperation to some modified form of the old native laws, surely no longer ought we to hesitate to make a definite change. For take even our civil courts; these we were confident could not fail to be successful. What has occurred? They are a complete curse to the people, bringing about endless litigation, and involving gross injustice to the poor, owing to their expense. Our land laws: these are found to be utterly ruinous, not in one part of India alone but in many, driving the cultivators first into the hands of the money-lenders and then into gaol. Our educational system: of that it is needless to speak. So far, it is practically non-existent, save for the well-to-do. Our public works – but these come under another head more conveniently. Now all these objections to our existing methods are made, not by outsiders, but by tried and trained official Englishmen, who having been appointed to account for the mischiefs which have arisen, speak plainly of the baneful effects of our blunders, and themselves suggest a reversion to native plans, which we had discarded before as unsuited to the people. It is painful to read their confession that somehow our system does not work, and yet to find that the very men who honestly admit this are averse from the only possible remedy.

For now comes the most serious part of the matter. India is a poor country. We have been trying to enrich her, and this is how we have done it. In 1856, a year before the mutiny, the sum

119

of £23,000,000 was taken from the people of India for the purposes of government; in 1880, twenty-four years after, no less a sum than £68,000,000 was taken from them for the same purpose. Has India, then, become so much richer in the quarter of a century? There is no evidence to that effect; much the other way. We know from official reports and official protests that, light as the taxation may seem to us, it is heavier than the people of India can bear. Any increase would be – I know no authority to the contrary of that – politically dangerous. The salt tax – levied, bear in mind, to the tune of 700 per cent *ad valorem* – interferes with the consumption of that necessary of life most seriously; whilst no less a man than the late Lord Lawrence thought the murrains among the cattle which have been so frequent of late years were, in part at least, due to the want of salt owing to its excessive price.

But there is graver evidence than the death of cattle, the ever-increasing spread of famines, and consequent death of men. Famines are far more frequent than they were. In the last twenty-three years there have been not fewer than six serious famines, which have swept away millions of the people, and millions of cattle too. The last great famines – those of Bombay and Madras, and the North-West Provinces – were something terrible; not fewer certainly than 7,000,000 of people died of starvation and famine-fever between 1876 and 1879 in those provinces. This is the worst famine of which there is any record whatever; and it occurred, not in the India of old time, with difficult communications, tottering Governments, indifferent and careless administrations; but in the India of today, with a powerful Central Government, with railroads and highways, canals and irrigation works – to say nothing of money freely poured forth to save these people from their dreadful fate. But this was an exceptional affair, it may be said; there was some phenomenal drought all over the country; the rains ceased, the whole land was barren. Drought no doubt there was, but by no means of inordinate severity, and this alone would not have accounted for the fearful mortality. Nowadays, sad to say, our people – the greater part of the 200,000,000 we are responsible for – are living nearer, and ever nearer, to the limit of starvation; thus what in happier periods would have been a scarcity, now deepens into a serious famine. And the main causes for this miserable state of things are not far to seek.

The total net revenue of the Government of India raised from the many and various races under our rule does not exceed £38,000,000 a year, after making deductions for the cost of collection. This revenue so raised cannot safely be increased: the mass of the people are, as has been said, taxed up to the hilt. But year after year we take out of the country agricultural produce to the amount of £20,000,000 at the very lowest estimate, to bring to us here in England, in order to pay interest, pensions, and home charges, for which there is no commercial return.

Now just think for a moment what this means. It means that this very year we Englishmen are taking from the people of India, for European rule and the use of European capital, more than we have ever taken: it means that this amounts to more than the total land revenue of all British India – to more than half the net income from all sources as calculated above. Yet India is a poor country is a very poor country, as Indian officials tell us. And this is how we "develop" it. We drain away from the country that produce which might be so beneficially employed by our fellow subjects; and then we beat our breasts when famine comes, and call out to Providence to wipe off those spots on the sun which somehow or other do all the mischief.

What cowardly pretence is this. The truth lies open to all. We are ruining India because our upper and middle classes will persist in exacting from its people agricultural produce to pay interest, home charges, and pensions. No country in the world, not blessed with virgin soil of exceptional fertility, could possibly stand such a drain without exhaustion. The real effect of this drain once fully grasped, all talk even about the uncertain opium revenue, about the grinding salt tax, about the mischievous licence and stamp tax, becomes idle; for by this constant demand we are draining away the very life-blood of our people. What would Englishmen say if the whole agricultural rent of the country went over to France every year, because we had French prefects in every county, and French money had built our railroads and excavated our canals? Yet the agricultural rent of England is a mere fleabite in comparison with the drain from India, the relative wealth of the two countries being taken into account.

"But then," say investors, "the railroads, the canals, have increased the wealth of India; we must have interest from our money, no matter how many are starved every now and then to pay us. To argue otherwise would be communism, confiscation again. It is absurd to forego interest to keep people alive." Well, have the railroads increased the wealth of India? Are the numberless foreigners employed a burden or the reverse? The matter really requires but little consideration. Railroads do but transport wealth from one point to another more conveniently than common roads. They themselves, make no wealth, neither do they add to that already in existence. Those who find the capital deduct a certain proportion of the produce transferred for the payment of working expenses and interest. Now if this proportion of produce remains in the country, and is paid to natives, it is still at hand to feed the people; but if it is loaded on board ships, as jute, cotton, or indigo, and sent to a foreign country to pay interest on capital [which as we have seen, means the wages of past (unpaid) labour, now owned by those who neither toil nor spin], then so much wealth is taken clean out of that country, never to reappear or to return to fertilize the soil. There are new colonies, no doubt, which can afford to pay this toll to foreigners, because the application of labour to virgin soil is exceedingly profitable, though even in that case the drain is often more injurious than it seems at the time. But in the case of India the result is disastrous from the first. Interest is taken away, and Europeans are paid high salaries, alike in famine and in plenty, in drought and in flood. Moreover, much more than £20,000,000 have been thus paid away under the guarantee which have never been earned at all. Losing railways have consequently been made profitable investments to home capitalists by the truly beneficent intervention of their own Government. Railways therefore in India, worked by Europeans at a high salary, and paying interest on the money borrowed by sending agricultural produce out of the country, are very different from railways here with us in England. This has now been acknowledged. Borrowing out of India is seen to be most injurious; and yet the country is getting deeper and ever deeper into debt for public works, and the exhausting drain is being increased by the employment of more Europeans.

The truth is that, built with the best possible intentions, the public works of India are a burden on the people. Eager to enrich the country and yet to derive advantage from it, our proceedings for the last three-and-twenty years have been harmful and ruinous in the highest degree. This is no secret. The most important officials at the India Office know it well. The fearful effect of the drain from India has been the subject of more than one grave confidential memorandum, as well as of protests from Indian Finance Ministers, who, however, could not see themselves that the construction of unremunerative public works out of borrowed money was ruinous. But such is capitalism – selfishness so ingrained that five per cent. per annum cannot possibly be wrong, though millions may starve because it must be punctually paid. We have lent nearly £250,000,000 to India, and must have our return, though the people had no voice whatever in the borrowing, and now begin to feel only too sadly that their substance is being taken from them, they scarcely know how.

But this drain must be stanched; the taxation must be lowered; more natives must be employed. England, in short, must rise to the level of her great responsibilities, and take order with the ex-officials who pour forth optimist harangues in praise of their own administrative capacity. For hear what all agricultural experts say. With one accord Mr. Buck, Mr. Harman, and Mr. Robertson declare that the soil of India is undergoing steady and permanent deterioration – that it will support fewer men and fewer bullocks as years pass by. Mr. Robertson puts the deterioration at not less than thirty per cent. in thirty years. Thirty per cent. less produce per acre in thirty years! Who can wonder? The produce of the earth is taken away to be brought over here, to an increasing extent, and there is now less manure than ever to put into the soil. At the same time the destruction of the forests for railway sleepers and fuel has, as in the United States and Australia, most seriously affected the climate for the worse. Drought and floods alternate in districts where formerly the rainfall was beneficial and equable. Such is the foresight of capital in India – the care of our civilization of to-day for the civilization of the human beings of tomorrow. From all provinces comes the same sad cry. From the North-West and from Oude, from Bombay as well as from Madras, from large tracts of Bengal, and even from the Punjab, one mournful story is heard; the land does not, as of old bring forth of its abundance; there is no blessing on the crops in our day. A deteriorated race of men, an inferior description of bullocks, bear witness to the truth of what they say.

So serious did all this seem, so fearful was the famine period of 1876-79, that Mr. James Caird was sent out to India as a Special Famine Commissioner, with the ready consent of both parties in the State, to examine, as the ablest English agricultural expert, into the condition of our noble dependency. He returned to tell us that unless we change our system a great catastrophe is inevitable. Catastrophe is easily written, but Mr. Caird evidently used the word in no light sense. After an elaborate investigation of the state of things, he too came to the conclusion that the soil of India is deteriorating, whilst the population is increasing in certain districts, so that the people live in perpetual semi-starvation. The very next famine period may therefore bring with it an economical cataclysm beside which even the great Irish destruction will sink into insignificance. Mr. Irwin prepares us in Oude for similar fearful trouble; Mr. Connell from the North-West Provinces takes up the tale. But Mr. Caird's earnest protest has, so far, produced no effect; so what should they avail? Even Mr. W.W. Hunter, the Director-General of Indian Statistics, and a year ago advocate of the interests of the Indian bureaucracy and capitalists at home, even he, alarmed at last by his own very inaccurate figures, tells us that at least 40,000,000 of the people for whose welfare we are responsible – 100,000,000 would be nearer the mark – are going through life on insufficient food. Nay, more; he shows that the Mogul Emperors raised far more than twice the revenue we now get out of India, for six generations, without exhausting the country, whilst we who drain away the produce cannot take our present revenue without a great risk of collapse. By the side of this drain, and the consequent deterioration of the soil, helped on by denudation, all the rest of our blunders, great as they are, are mere child's-play. Another famine period is even now approaching, no preparations have been made to meet it, and how far the inordinate cost of the Afghan wars has crippled our Indian exchequer is not even yet fully known.

Thus on every side the prospect is gloomy and overcast, and in the opinion of the ablest observers we are drawing nearer and nearer to an almost overwhelming disaster. Year after year we take from India agricultural produce which she cannot spare, because we are masters of the country, and, paying ourselves handsomely all round, leave those who depend upon us for safety to perish from want. Whilst we are disputing about the defence of the empire we ourselves are preparing its ruin, only to learn the truth too late: the knocking will come through the darkness from without – the murder within will be done. Let then the sun of English justice arise and shine – outshine all the glories of the East; let a message of mercy, whose wings are as silver wings and her feathers as gold, go forth from the people of England to the many races and nations under their rule, saying to all that, though they have ills of their own to suffer from and endless sorrows to bear, they would not that others should be made poorer or more miserable for them. So as death shall close our eyelids in never-ending slumber, we may feel that countless millions have some share of happiness which but for us they would have lacked, some joy and contentment which but for us they never would have known.

For the alternative course lies open before us once more. There are in India, as in Ireland and at home, two policies, the one of mock freedom and real oppression, the other of beneficent government and steady progress. Strange that having tried both methods in India, we should as a nation stick to the failure and discard the success. Wherever native administration has had free play under gentle European guidance, there we have seen prosperity and contentment spring up and endure. In Travancore and Baroda, in Mysore and Hyderabad, wherever English influence has been confined to supporting upright native rule, the change has been marvellous for the better, though the tendency even then is to interfere too much by the introduction of Western ideas. Still it is not European administration that is necessarily ruinous: that we have seen in numerous instances. It is not that public works are not highly beneficial. But when European agency and public works are alike overdone; when foreign soldiers and foreign systems are imposed upon the population to an extent which savours of the very fanaticism of so-called improvement, then, as we see, the result is starvation, ruin, and death, a famine-stricken people, and an exhausted soil.

The recent return of Mysore to native administration

after fifty years of European rule is, we may hope, of good omen for the future. Our task now is to cut down the European establishments in every-possible way – to curtail the home charges, even if we have to reduce the rate of interest arbitrarily by one half and take some portion of the pensions on to our own shoulders. This money that is now taken is not ours, and no native has ever voted a single rupee of it to us. The enormous expense of the European army must likewise be curtailed, and a very different policy from that of suspicion and hauteur adopted towards the native princes. We have, in fact, to prepare the many peoples of India for self-government, by a process of decentralization, by building up the old States again wherever possible, and by removing the crowd of Europeans who now eat out the prosperity of the country. Let any man consider. No such system as that which we now foster could by any possibility succeed. The old Mogul rulers were wrong-headed enough in many ways, but they were not such fools as to think they could govern India from Samarcand and in accordance with Mussulman prejudice, or that they could dispense with the assistance of the able Hindoo administrators in the management of their provinces. Akber was perhaps the greatest monarch that the East ever produced, yet he relied – and as the event showed, wisely relied – upon the noble rajah Toder Mull to reorganize his finances. With us Toder Mull, the most masterly financier beyond all comparison that has ever had control of the Indian exchequer, would have been "a damned nigger accountant, who would keep writing to the papers." Such incapacity to appreciate the abilities of our own subjects, let us remember— such eagerness to crush down rather than to raise up – such sad indifference to the ruin being wrought in our own territory, when close at hand countries equally under our control, but managed by natives, are flourishing and prosperous – such strange determination not to understand, I say, will gain us but a doubtful reputation for foresight with those who come after, even if it do not involve ourselves in ruin.

127

But if, on the other hand, we resolve to make the necessary changes at once, and to restore to the natives, in some degree at least, the control of their own Governments and their own property, then India may more than repay us for our sympathy and goodwill. There, directly or indirectly under our rule, are 250,000,000 of the human race, who, weary as they are of waiting for fair treatment, would recognize with joyous loyalty a determined effort to relieve them from the excessive pressure of foreign government, and the ruinous drain for foreign payments, which now impoverish them more and more. This assuredly is no party question; but those who profit by India's ruin will scarcely of their own motion make the sacrifices needful to restore her prosperity. It is to the mass of Englishmen, then, to the great democracy of this country, that the peoples of India must now appeal for justice. Represented fairly here at home, they might hope to secure their long-delayed hearing, and with that hearing consideration for their wrongs. Here too, I say once more, the right course is that which is best also for our own people. Let the people of India but grow in wealth, as they would under any fair conditions of existence, with but slight supervision from us, and the exchange of their products for ours would be far more advantageous than the continuous impoverishment which disenables them from making purchases. On every ground, therefore, of humanity, morality, self-interest, future credit, and ordinary common sense, we ought not longer to postpone the necessary reorganization. But our present parliamentary system has proved quite inadequate to cope with this great crisis. If India is to be retained at all, she must have a direct voice in her own administration, as well in England as in India.

128

Chapter VII The Colonies

There is happily one portion of our empire which is almost entirely free from the political difficulties we encounter elsewhere. The drawbacks to our great self-governed colonies are common to our age and civilization; their advantages are peculiar to themselves. Notwithstanding the mistakes of both political parties in dealing with South Africa – mistakes which have, to a great extent, overclouded the prospect in that particular region – the colonies are, and will remain, the chief mainstay of Anglo-Saxon dominion outside these islands, when India has returned to native rule, and our other dependencies are held rather as a duty than as contributing to our power. With them, indeed, and the United States, lies the future expansion of our race. For although the Americans were driven into hostility more than a century ago, we may still hope that in time to come the great English-speaking democracies of England, Australia, and North America, may find ground for a common understanding, which will enable them to secure peace and justice; throughout the civilized world, by the overwhelming force they could array against any aggressor. This, however, is for the moment no more than a pleasant vision. [1]

The possibility of a closer connexion with our colonies is an immediate practical business. On this point too, fortunately, men who differ most widely on other questions are often agreed. Taught by the disastrous result of the attempt to tyrannize over the North American colonists, we have carried the doctrine of self-government almost further than the colonists themselves wished. Not content with granting them the most complete home rule, we have at times repulsed their advances towards a closer union, and, on the other hand, wronged our poorer classes by handing over the entire administration of an almost limitless unoccupied territory to the handful of people who first settled there. But even so the result is surely in marked contrast to our relations with Ireland. No portion of our dominions are so loyal to the British connexion at this very time, none so anxious that England should rightfully maintain her position in the world, as the colonists. Left to solve their own social and political problems, they turn naturally to the mother country to keep alive the ideal of a greater political action than any which can be hoped for from mere separation and local ambition. And this feeling grows even at the time when absentees are being denounced, and the power of democracy gains ground each day. There, as at home, centralization and decentralization are working themselves out; though, by the mistake of not maintaining a federal union, great difficulties are now encountered in bringing together colonies which ought never to have lost the common tie, even on matters which could manifestly be handled best by all collectively.

There can be no greater contrast between the relation which Canada now bears to the United Kingdom than that of the North American colonies, when they fought for independence. In that case we insisted upon the right to tax without permitting the colonists the right of representation. Now we have given Canada not only self-government, but the right to impose almost prohibitive duties on our own goods. That this need not have occurred had a better understanding been kept up with the colonists, and free-trade, when commenced, enacted as the law for all self-governed portions of the empire, we can scarcely doubt. The history of Canada, however, since the separation of the American colonies, is creditable to her and to the home country. At first sight it would have seemed impossible that the French colonies of Lower Canada, conquered by a people with whom their nation was at perpetual war, should ever have come to be loyal to the English Crown. But the consideration shown for their language, creed, and customs, the steady determination not to interfere with their local rule, gradually won over the French settlers, until at the present time they are as devoted to

130

the British connexion as any portion of the population of English descent. Troubles at times there have been with the English colonists, and rather more than forty years ago a rebellion was threatened. Yet all settled down; and now it seems that the Dominion of Canada has before her as fine a career in the future as the more energetic democracy on the other side of the border. That the withdrawal of our troops was brought about in a most unmannerly fashion, and in such wise as to offend the best instincts of the Canadians – that also Lord Carnarvon's plan of federation was rather premature, and carried by doubtful means, have not changed the sentiments of the colonists towards the mother country.

Incorporation with the United States would leave less of freedom for natural expansion than there is at present under England's light rule. A race of sturdy sober-going men and women have grown up in that rude Canadian climate, who will carry on the best traditions of English Government side by side with the great Republic. There, in the great expanse of the Far West, lies an opening for those who, in the coming changes here at home, may think they see their way to a wider field, still under the name and in connexion with the old country. In Canada, even more than in the United States, the natural inclination of our race for the sea manifests itself. The 4,000,000 who make up the Dominion of Canada own the fourth largest mercantile marine in the world. As, also, the new continental railroad is pushed forward to the Pacific slope, the splendid region of British Columbia will be opened up to colonization, and yet another connexion made with the English colonies in the South Pacific.

Nor, when the distance by sea is spoken of, and the impossibility of a permanent connexion insisted upon, should we forget that Canada and the other colonies of the Atlantic slope are nearer to us to-day than Aberdeen or Cork were a century ago. Canada is now wholly self-supporting, costs the people of England not one farthing of expenditure, whilst the increasing power of democracy would find a help and offer valuable assistance to a similar growth with us at home. The Dominion will, we may hope, as time passes on, bind together closer the various settlements. Already the Parliament at Ottawa – sitting in the finest block of buildings on the American continent – worthily represents the Federal Union of a magnificent group of peoples. Let them also find representation here in England, and thus bring to bear upon all international arrangements the ever-increasing force of a united democracy of English-speaking peoples. At the crisis of the Eastern question when it seemed as if England might be involved in continental warfare, the Canadians were not slow to offer their assistance in a cause where their own interests were in no way involved. Surely it is for the great mass of the people of England to hold out their hands in fellowship to those who wish nothing better than to work together on the same lines for the strengthening and improvement of all. There is something in great ideas which vivifies and enlarges the national imagination. We here at home have indeed much to carry out ere we can achieve our own full government of ourselves, or place ourselves on the same level which the Canadians have already happily attained to in many respects. Reason the more that we should endeavour to make common cause in the direction of further progress.

But if this applies to Canada, still more true is it of the Australian colonies and New Zealand. These colonies are the growth of the present generation. In the last thirty years they have sprung up from mere settlements to be great and prosperous communities. In Australia – Victoria and New South Wales, South Australia, Queensland, and West Australia, form a group of states unsurpassed in any part of the world for energy, enterprise, and growing consideration for the education and well-being of the rising generation. That the distribution of wealth is here also sadly faulty is indeed too certain. In

Melbourne and Sydney, cities large out of all proportion to the population engaged in agriculture or mining, the contrast between the wealth of the few and the poverty of the many, is at times very serious. Here, too, is felt the alternation of inflation and stagnation consequent upon our capitalist system, and the large capitalists, either English or native, are gradually acquiring excessive preponderance. But the possibility of a man taking himself out of the wage-earning class is, of course, as in Canada and the United States, far greater than in England. The abundance of virgin soil, the rapid increase of wealth in proportion to the population, keep wages at a higher level than in old countries. Both politically and socially, however, the Australian colonies are passing through a phase in their history which is of the highest importance, and corresponds to similar changes here at home. In purely political matters the democracy is increasing in strength day by day; but unfortunately these colonies have not, until of late years, had anything to compare to the admirable school system of America which should bring the whole population within reach of education. This, however, is being remedied; and in Victoria, the most democratic colony of all, the people are beginning to learn that a sober combination to deal with existing difficulties – which may well perplex the ablest statesman – is in the long-run better for the interests of all than a hasty agitation which overthrows confidence in present arrangements without substituting anything in their place. Those who fasten their attention on Victoria, and declaim against the folly of a democracy because it favours protection, conveniently forgot that New South Wales, where the people are equally masters, is in favour of free trade, and South Australia shows a growing tendency in the same direction. Nothing, indeed, is more absurd than to gauge the political intelligence of a country by such a test. If protection can keep up the relative wages of the mass of the working people above the level which they will obtain under free trade, then beyond all question protection is, on the whole, the policy best suited to the welfare of the mass of that community. Theorists who reason as if the only object of all human society were to make the rich richer and the poor poorer would, of course, not admit even that.

But it may be reasonably allowed as absurd that colonies founded by men of the same nation, and living under the same government, in the same territory, should deliberately set up tariffs against one another, and against the mother country. This is what we see in Australia, and it shows clearly how important a better understanding is between the various colonies on matters which concern the interests of all. The difficulty of bringing about a federation in Australia, even on this simple matter of customs, seems insuperable. Time after time have representatives met, but on each occasion have separated without coming to any definite arrangement. Local interests and local ambitions shut out the view of the general advantage which would be gained by a closer understanding. But the completion of a railroad between Sydney and Melbourne, and the rapid extension of the other Australian railways, must bring this question again to the front. It may be that the solution will be found in that wider federation which, without in any way sacrificing the local administration, may bring about the full representation of Australia in a general council where the interests of all will be fully considered. There are, in these days, many matters which can be better settled when dealt with as a whole than when regarded piecemeal, and few can doubt that such enterprises as the railways and public works of Australia could be better and more cheaply handled together than separately.

In these Australian colonies also, and particularly in New Zealand, may be seen the system of State management carried out under the most democratic form of government. Railways, posts, telegraphs, public works, schools, public lands, are all entirely under the control of the bureaux appointed by the

State, and managed by a responsible Minister. Where the appointments also are kept clear of political influence, the system works well. There are temptations to grave jobbery, doubtless, but they are kept under restraint by universal publicity; and the mass of the population have abundant opportunities of making themselves felt. A graver danger than any arising from over-officialism is that of over-borrowing from the mother country. In New Zealand especially this danger is very great. Not only is the Government largely pledged to pay the produce of the 400,000 colonists to home lenders, but the settlers themselves have pledged their resources to an enormous extent to English capitalists. These vast payments out of the country for money borrowed can scarcely go on for ever. Labour expended on virgin soil will no doubt produce enormously; but slack times come even there, and the difficulties which we have seen in India will be reproduced on a smaller scale. This vast tribute, in the shape of interest on money lent, which the English colonists have to transmit out of their labour to the mother country, is one of the least pleasant features of the colonial connexion.

It may be that under a better arrangement the colonists in all our great free-governed dependencies will be able to combine with the mother country for the more adequate development of their magnificent territories, in the interest of the whole of the federated portions of our empire. In their temperate climate, and with their unrivalled soil – in Canada, Australia, Tasmania, and New Zealand – millions on millions of our race might find happiness and comfort, which would re-act upon the welfare of our people at home. As our home arrangements undergo modification, we ought to carry with us the people of the colonies in aiding to bring about, without disturbance or bloodshed, a more equitable distribution of wealth than that which now we see. Those who desire to leave our shores to try a fresh life in another country, might then feel sure, not of the coddling of a maternal government, but of assistance, encouragement, and capital, where now all these are lacking. The great disparity between the sexes in England in one direction, and in the colonies in the other, alone shows how faultily the present arrangements have worked. It is with a view to bringing about a more complete understanding on all such questions, a regulation of the mere *laissez-faire* system which up till now has found favour, that a nearer connexion is so essential. Friendly democracies can always help each other. They have no real ground of mutual distrust. But when we see in the United States such misery as that produced by the late stagnation; when we know that in New South Wales, Victoria, and New Zealand, men were thrown out of work and clamouring for employment, though millions of unoccupied fertile land lay at their disposal all round them, then it becomes more clearly apparent than ever how mischievous is the system which refuses to make the most of such enormous advantages, and supposes that stagnation and depression are really inevitable because those who hold the capital choose to make it so.

It is because social matters are kept so carefully in the background, and the real producers of wealth, whether in England, Ireland, or abroad, are shut out from comparing notes on matters which so nearly concern them, that these serious errors are made. Even as it is the colonies, with their marvellous power of recovery, have been our best customers, and have enabled the English working class at home to pass through the long period of crisis with less of pressure than would otherwise have been felt. Here, even in business, where sentiment is said to have no play, we find the trade follows the flag – that men prefer to deal with their own people. Surely those who are in favour of a unity of all peoples, who hold that in the near future the men who have hitherto worked for others will see that in common action lies the hope for humanity, cannot fail ere long to understand that the first step towards this great end must be a closer and yet closer union of peoples of the same race, language, and political traditions, working together for the good of all portions of that noble federation. Leaving freedom to all, and enforcing none – holding up before us a high ideal in which all may share and all may find full development – thus, and thus only, shall we gather them in.

But it is not merely in relation to their own individual interests that it would be of the highest importance that our great democratic communities beyond the sea should be represented. Difficulties affecting all portions of the empire have to be considered, which can never obtain proper attention save by the personal discussion of those who have a direct interest in their wise settlement. The questions of tariff and trade have already been spoken of. No complete arrangements on these heads can possibly be arrived at so long as the hide-bound bureaucrats of the Colonial Office, with their encrusted traditions of meddling and muddling, have full swing. Only when men see for themselves that local selfishness can fitly be merged in a greater and more enlightened common interest, will they abandon ideas which they have adopted almost as an evidence of free judgment. A Customs Union of the British Empire will be the outcome of the representation of our colonies in the Great Council which will take the place of our present worn-out second chamber. Or it may be even that we shall follow the French system, and invite colonies to send representatives to the popular House, when local business has been properly handed over to local authorities. Whichever course may be adopted, there is a growing opinion, both in the colonies and in England, that in such representation lies the true solution of many problems which now seem most thorny. A complete Union thus brought about could scarcely fail to have a peaceful influence on the whole civilized world. Such an overwhelming combination of naval strength as could then be relied upon, could be made by no conceivable alliance of despotic powers.

This, however, brings us at once to the question of general defence, which is now being discussed by a Royal Commission. On that Commission the colonies are inadequately represented, yet it is of the last importance that they should enter completely into any plans that may be suggested. For on the due ordering of our Imperial defences, and the security of our lines of communication, can we alone depend for maintaining in time of trouble that connexion with our countrymen across the sea, and for the certainty of obtaining our food supplies, which are essential not only to our influence but to our safety. These matters have been sadly neglected under the happy-go-lucky *régime* of the past twenty or thirty years. Men who are always looking to throw off what they call the "burden of empire," regardless of the help and encouragement we can obtain in coming political changes from the democracies of our own race, naturally looked askance at any measures which should tend to unite and not to separate, to bring together and not to drive away. It is well that at this particular time another view should be taken. By a careful organization of our resources, and a judicious strengthening of the many ports we possess, it would be made quite impossible for any enemy or enemies to interfere seriously with our affairs even in time of war, whilst the denunciation of the Declaration of Paris would make us more powerful than we ever were before. In these days coal and coaling-stations, the opportunity to go into port and refit at all times, are essential. And these advantages we possess to such an extent, that it may almost be said that all the rest of the world together could not rival us. In the Atlantic and Pacific, in European waters and the China seas, from the Cape of Good Hope to Cape Horn, and from the British islands to Australia and India, we hold a chain of posts which will enable us to exercise at the fitting moment an almost overwhelming pressure, if in time of peace we take the means to prepare for any difficulty. Halifax and Vancouver's Island, Bermuda and the Falkland Islands, Gibraltar, Malta, and Aden, Sydney,

Melbourne, King George's Sound, and Auckland, to say nothing of the Indian ports, and scarcely less valuable possessions elsewhere, such as Hong-Kong, Fiji, and the Mauritius, constitute an array of maritime citadels which, maintained in proper defence by our ourselves and our colonies, must, in conjunction with a fleet proportioned to our maritime interests, render future naval war against us almost impossible. Nor should we hold or exercise this truly enormous power for our own selfish advantage. English ports are open to the ships of all nations without let or hindrance; we throw open to the world the advantages we possess, asking nothing in return. Here, then, when fully represented, our colonists may fairly take their share in arranging with us the defence of the common interest, and organizing the national defence.

Still more necessary, however, is colonial help in considering the bearing of treaties which we may negotiate with foreign powers, or the action which the colonists themselves may take in their own interest. At present there is no special consideration given to the effect which may be produced on our existing artificial system by any fresh arrangement so far as it affects colonies or colonists, and our greatest dependency counts for still less in such matters; whilst as to the colonists themselves, it is sufficient to note their action with regard to the Chinese to recognize at once that questions may arise which can only be dealt with from the point of view of general interest. This Chinese question is indeed one which by itself needs the gravest consideration, as a political, social, and international problem of the greatest difficulty. Here we are in fact threatened with a conflict of races and civilization, the like of which has never yet been seen on the face of the planet. China has awakened from her long sleep of centuries, and is fast breaking from her isolation, and entering into the full stream of the political and social life of our times. What the results of this may be no man can foretell. A people who have been civilized for ages, who yet retain vigour, capacity, and physical qualities, whose bearing on the future we do not yet fully understand, are now absorbing the newest truths of Western investigators. The effect upon us so far has been to bring the industrious Chinese, with their ideas of individualism only modified by their secret societies, into direct competition with our own colonists. There are thousands on thousands of Chinamen under our rule in the East alone, and as workmen and merchants they are most formidable rivals. But with the emigration to the free-governed colonies and America a new feature begins. Our colonists positively will not put up with them, any more than the Americans will. At this very time the people of British Columbia, as well as the colonies of Australia, have decided to keep out the Chinese. They are to our modern industrial colonists what shells are at sea – missiles to be kept out, at any cost to theory or beauty of design. But the result is at once seen to be serious. It is the recognition of a perturbing element in all calculations – of an incapacity on the part of our race to face a nation of protectionists who regard themselves as mere passers-by in every country they enter. That our colonists should have the right to tax every Chinaman who lands, surely carries with it the right of Chinese to tax every Englishman who lands in China. As our relations with China grow, and these points come more prominently forward, the absolute necessity for some general understanding will become apparent. Perhaps ere another generation has passed away the question of our relation to China will completely dwarf all others in importance. Meantime the commercial connexion between Australia and Asia is rapidly growing; and in view of the unfitness of the northern portion of that great island-continent for colonization by men of our race, it is even possible that immigrants from India or China may find place in that vast unpeopled region.

These, however, are the possibilities of the future. What most concerns us now is, to lay the foundation of a cordial understanding between all portions of our great colonial empire – to bring together on the wider field of a wide-reaching policy of the commonwealth those who in their own several spheres, are striving to bring about a better social and political system than that which now presses upon all portions of the empire, though less in the colonies than elsewhere. The natural and wholesome pride of a Canadian, an Australian, or a New Zealander in the growing greatness of his country, need in no way be irreconcilable with a deep love for the old home, and a yet higher pride in sharing in a general improvement which shall embrace and welcome all. The Anglo-Saxon race, which has shown the world how to reconcile freedom and order with steady progress, can by combination and determined effort secure for themselves and their children the leadership in the social changes and reforms which are close at hand. Those great democracies of English-speaking peoples, who now have complete control over their own affairs, will find that in permanent union with the more ancient democracy of England lies the best hope of securing the fullest development in the future.

Notes

1. "Blood is thicker than water," said Admiral Farragut when he stood by our sailors in the China seas. Years later, after the grand old man had been the soul of the Northern navy during the Civil War, he was in port in the Mediterranean with his wooden flagship. A fleet of British ironclads was there at the same time. As he weighed anchor and sailed out to sea, the English ships also left their moorings and made two lines for him to pass through. The compliment was wholly unlooked-for, but it thoroughly expressed the feelings of the nation towards that noble seaman.

Chapter VIII Foreign Affairs

The relation which England should bear to the nations of the Continent of Europe, and the action which ought to be taken in reference to foreign policy generally, would be very summarily settled by one party among us. Non-intervention is their sole idea of the management of such affairs. Let others do what they like to or with one another, we will severely mind our own business, look after our trade, and, secure behind the silver streak, amass money – for the comfortable classes of course – to our hearts' content. Thus the individual selfishness, upon which they are content to rely absolutely for all management at home, is fitly supplemented by a still more thorough collective selfishness applied to affairs abroad.

Capital is timid, it is said, peace is our greatest interest, intervention means, sooner or later, war or threat of war. A soldier or a sailor therefore, in the opinion of these gentlemen, ought to be scouted as a pariah, though, as all save fanatics can see, our army and navy are as natural portions of our industrial organism in the present state of international morality and economical development, as our custom-house or excise. Only stand aside, such is the argument, and no one will harm you. A purely trading power will arouse no jealousies; and Europe will see in England a country which, in the plenitude of its strength, steps aside from all save commercial transactions, and is content to figure simply as a pattern to others. Now, few would doubt that if all were like-minded in this matter – if the lion of greed could indeed lie down with the lamb of wealth outside him, that here is the true industrial future for the human race. But we are, alas! far from such a happy state of things. No nation in existing conditions can thus safely boycott itself, without grave risk of being boycotted, or perhaps preyed upon, by others. And we, of all countries in the world, are the least capable of secluding ourselves, and enriching ourselves whilst others look on. Our flag floats on every sea; our trade competes with every nation; our absolutely necessary supplies, without which we should starve, come to us from far and near. [1]

A commercial country owning such extended territory is more open to attack than any other; and even on the ground of simple selfishness, some alliances should be made, and some preparations maintained against danger. But there are higher reasons even than those of expediency for taking part in the politics of the world. A great country has moral duties, as a man has moral duties; and these are not confined to simple business relations and trading for gain. We are, or might be, the leaders and protectors of freedom, independence, and true liberty in Europe, as we were in the time of the Great Protector. Our power, properly organized, and wielded with the consent of a united people, may suffice at no distant date to turn the scale in that great struggle between industrialism and militarism, between tyranny and freedom, perhaps between barbarism and civilization, now threatening on the continent. To stand aloof finally when such issues as these are being debated is not, as I venture to think, the nature of my countrymen. They have often fought in times gone by to save others from foreign domination; it maybe that in the near future a still greater task will be theirs.

The history of the modern connexion of England with continental affairs, may be said to begin with the accession of William III. That long policy of secret negotiations carried on by Elizabeth with the Protestant populations of Europe, had involved us in war with Spain; and the policy of the Stuarts had, after Cromwell's short and glorious period of supremacy, made England subservient to France. But these wars and alliances had really as little to do with the events which followed, as the old wars in France under the Plantagenets. With William III, however, began that bitter rivalry with France which thenceforward became the mainspring of English foreign policy for at least five generations. Rivalry no doubt existed between Englishmen and Frenchmen when the Prince of Orange came to the throne, but thenceforward it spread from the people to the Governments, and the fierce struggle which followed spread to all quarters of the globe. William III, in fact, began a settled policy of interference in European State politics in the interest of Holland and Germany, as distinct from any cause which called us to take the field on our own account. As a consequence we were driven to fight foreign battles by means of subsidies and mercenary troops, instead of trusting to our power at sea, where lies our real strength.

For, strange to say, it never occurred to either the Plantagenets, the Tudors, or the Stuarts that it would redound to our credit and influence to carry on campaigns on land with German soldiers at England's expense. William III, however, commenced the system, because it aided the policy of his own country laid down by himself – that of persistent opposition to Louis XIV and the French. The result has been a crushing load of debt, permanently imposed for foreign objects on the English people. For the House of Brunswick, confirmed and greatly extended the mischievous policy introduced by the Dutch king; and henceforth England became the citadel of German resistance to French attacks upon Germany. We no longer had a continental policy of our own; every step taken had reference to the relations and intrigues of other Powers, who came to look upon England and English Ministers as necessary supports of a system of international war and jealousy, with which, as a matter of fact, the English people had nothing whatever to do. The unquestioned facts that we fought bravely, won battle after battle, and acquired some magnificent colonies, are mere incidents of this State-system which blind us to the true bearing of the policy itself.

Had not the Dutch and German elements become paramount in the guidance of our foreign relations, there was no such necessary antagonism to France as has been pretended. Lord Chatham himself, whose management of our external affairs was the wonder of Europe, was vehemently opposed to the "German War," which, having once commenced, not even his genius could clear us from. Thus England was dragged along at the heels of Frederick II the most unscrupulous adventurer who ever made a kingdom out of a province, and we of to-day have the privilege of paying, in the shape of interest on the national debt, for the position which Prussia holds in Europe. This went on, notwithstanding protests from patriotic men against this ruinous squandering of the resources of the country, until the time of the French Revolution, when our antagonism to France, already pronounced enough, was still further aggravated by the calculated panic of the governing and well-to-do classes. With the internal affairs of France we had no concern; and the mass of the people of England sympathized with the men who had overturned the meanest, and at the same time most galling tyranny that could oppress an agricultural people. The loss of the American Colonies, when Germans and Indians were used to shoot down and scalp men who were fighting for their rights, had opened the eyes of the poorer classes to the real bearing of the vicious mercenary system. A magnificent heritage had been lost, because the men at the head of affairs set aside the advice of Englishmen like Chatham and Burke, to pander to the prejudices of a German king and the aristocrats around him. France had now learnt something from America; and there was more admiration than ill-feeling to begin with on our side of the Channel.

But in all this the rulers of that day saw – and rightly saw – a grave danger to themselves. The rupture with France was made unavoidable by the counsel and support extended to her invaders. Once involved in the anti-revolutionary fever, nothing was easier than to inflame still further the national rivalry, until for nearly a generation the very name of Frenchman became obnoxious to English ears, and children grew up to be men believing that only by the destruction of France could England be made secure. The astounding career of Napoleon I, and the statecraft of his reactionary empire, gave our policy a further push forward in the same direction. England became the rallying-point of resistance to a military usurper, who evidently aimed at the dominance of Europe.

His answers to our persistent hostilities took the shape of a threat of invasion, and a continental blockade against English goods. The first of these two measures became hopeless after Nelson's crowning victory at Trafalgar. The second was rendered futile – though the fact is not generally known – by the friendly policy of the Ottoman Empire. The remarkable geographical configuration of that State gave us an advantage which Napoleon was unable to overcome. The Turks opened their numerous ports, and Europe was flooded with smuggled English goods. Thereupon the blockade became useless; Power after Power withdrew from the league, and we were relieved from further anxiety in regard to the most dangerous plan of campaign ever formulated against us. As a natural sequence of our long opposition to France, we were driven more and more into alliance with the despotic powers of Europe. Those armies which overthrew Napoleon, were as much intended for repression at home as to repel the foreign invader; and Europe was prepared by the Treaty of Vienna for the supremacy of the Holy Alliance. The great name associated with all this policy is that of Castlereagh, who bound us hand and foot to Russia, and made us little better than a hanger-on to the Holy Alliance itself. Thus for thirty years England was linked on the continent of Europe with powers whose very existence depended upon the denial of freedom to the peoples.

Upon this phase followed a modification rather than a change of policy. The extravagant pretensions of the Holy Alliance with reference to Spain, and the absurd claim of its members to regulate the internal affairs of every kingdom of

Europe, brought about the policy of which Canning became the chief exponent. This was the support of constitutionalism in Europe, as equally opposed to autocracy and to revolution. It was an attempt to trim between two irreconcilable opposites. Canning himself called into existence that remarkable New World to redress the balance of the Old which, since it first came above the political horizon in the House of Commons, has been wholly incapable of balancing even itself. The rest of the policy had as little solid foundation as this famous outburst. Constitutionalism did not thrive, in spite of English protection; and we gradually drifted into a defence of what appeared our most tangible, interest—that of the overland route to India.

Canning was followed by Palmerston and Russell. The episode of Navarino, which weakened Turkey without constituting a strong Greece, was merely a prelude to a definite championship of the integrity and independence of the Ottoman Empire, involving Lord Palmerston's Syrian policy, and eventually leading up to the Crimean War. Jealousy of France, and desire to maintain the balance of power, still had a great influence. But capitalism was now beginning to assert its sway, and plain Whig principles meant compromise at home and selfishness abroad. There was not even the violent old Toryism of Pitt and Castlereagh to rouse opposition or stir enthusiasm.

The shake of 1848 brought the weakness of this whole system into clear relief. Unpleasant people, who thought a dungeon smelt quite as dank under "moderate constitutionalism," as when kept exclusively at the service of autocrats, gave the constitutionalists many awkward misgivings. London at this time naturally became the headquarters of the constitutional monarchs, and the metropolitan bankers the custodians of their savings. We, however, in the struggle which followed, neither gained nor deserved the gratitude of either party. Opposed to autocracy, we showed a friendship for Hungary, for instance, which the horror of our middle classes for real revolution quickly induced us to betray. Matters were worse with Venice, Sardinia, and Sicily, when England deliberately abandoned people who had been induced by surreptitious assurances to rely upon her for assistance. "England wishes only for peace," Pasini wrote, bitterly, to Manin; and that summed up, not perhaps Lord Palmerston's own policy, but the policy of the capitalist class, now gaining power rapidly, and to which all Foreign Ministers have since been forced in some way to bow down.

But here, nevertheless, lay the true line for England. In 1848 she could have placed herself at the head of the enfranchised peoples of Europe, and lent her unrivalled naval power to support those who, with her assistance, could not have been subdued. The time however, was not ripe for so bold a policy; the dreaded principles of revolution were once more abroad. Chartism at home was affiliated to the accursed thing. So, without absolutely allying ourselves with the oppressors, Great Britain saw without regret the re-establishment of the autocracy, which to her self-seeking merchants was so far preferable to the rule of the people. Thus the general result of our moral support of constitutionalism and Liberal principles was the firm re-establishment of despotism in Europe. At this period too was shown fully that absolute agreement between Russia and Prussia which has been the key to continental policy since 1821. Russia came forward in 1848 as the protector of despotism in every country. Germany and Austria were completely under her thumb. Every petty princeling whose throne had been pulled from under him, stretched out his hands in prayer to the deity of St. Petersburg to set him up straight again; and Nicholas, to do him justice, did his king-making in fine old barbaric style. So long as these small fry, from the King of Prussia downward, obeyed his Imperial behests, and abstained from all tampering with liberalism or revolution he was content to support them for the mere gratification of the thing. The Power which held Poland could not afford that either

149

freedom or the rights of nationalities should be discussed in her neighbourhood. It was a revival of the policy of the early portion of the century, in a more pronounced shape. An armed barbarism lent its aid to all the reactionary influences in Europe, and Liberal England was content to stand aloof and wish well to the oppressed nationalities, without raising a hand to help them. Had a more far-seeing plan been adopted, the Crimean War, with its unfortunate alliance with the Second Empire in France might have been unnecessary.

Turkey was saved from Russia by that war, at the expense of thousands of lives and a hundred millions of money to this country. But for twenty years, though the Liberal party was almost continuously in office, no steps whatever were taken to reorganize the Ottoman Empire, or to help the better elements to organize themselves, whilst we lent the corrupt clique of Pashas at Constantinople tens of millions, which were squandered in corruption and debauchery. The close of the Crimean War, however, was signalized by a treaty, which could only have been reasonably accepted by us if we had been defeated instead of victorious. Hampered by our alliance with the Government, and not with the people of France, we were constrained to make peace practically on the terms which suited our ally. A step also was taken, without any reference to the people of England, by the two English Plenipotentiaries, which sacrificed the only important weapon that an essentially naval power like ourselves has in a continental war. The history of the deplorable surrender is even yet not fully known; its effect we shall only feel when we are again opposed – as we may be at any moment opposed – by a European coalition directed against us.

During the long wars with France under the Republic and Napoleon we held one great advantage, but for which we could scarcely have faced the combination which that great genius contrived to work up against us. This went by the name of Maritime Rights. Supreme on the ocean, and able to cover the seas with a swarm of privateers, the carrying trade of the world was at our mercy. The Right of Search was the point on which this power hinged. This meant that if neutral vessels were carrying our enemies' goods, we had the right, whether contraband of war or not, to stop those vessels and confiscate those goods. Thus we could rely upon our real arm, that which is given us by our geographical position and the hereditary capacity of our men – the knowledge and mastery of the sea. Time after time when the fortunes of the country had seemed at the lowest ebb, this power sufficed to turn the tide in our favour. Its possession made us a valuable ally to the most powerful continental state; whilst, as we have seen, with the friendly connivance of Turkey it enabled us to break up the famous continental blockade against our goods. Naturally this unequalled weapon, for a country of such wealth as ours, had been envied us by the continent ever since we began to use it, and constant efforts had been made by our rivals and enemies to deprive us of it. Up to the date of the Congress of Paris, however, all such pretensions had been scouted by English statesmen as absolutely inadmissible, and ruinous to our country. Nothing to the contrary of this had or has ever been shown. The cry of "free ships, free goods," had been raised by those who wished the downfall of England's influence; for once admitted, it reduced our fighting power to nothing.

All these facts notwithstanding, Lord Clarendon and Lord Cowley, acting in that spirit of the pure trading interest which had then become really paramount in English foreign politics, gave up by the Declaration of Paris, without argument, debate, or proper authority, those maritime rights which could alone enable the growing democracy of these lands to exercise due weight and influence in Europe. No such sacrifice has ever been made by any country. That we should permanently adhere to it is incredible. The United States was guilty of no such folly. Her statesmen declined to give up privateering, except under provisions which they knew would not be accepted. No long period can elapse before this whole question is again brought forward. When it is, the people of England should never cease to recall the fact that their position in the world awakens the jealousies of other nations, that these are the days of violent aggression and secret combinations, and that the weapon, the only weapon which nature has placed in our hands wherewith with perfect freedom to face and overcome the military despotisms of Europe, is that of being able to dominate the commerce of the globe.

Soon after the Treaty of Paris, the Indian Mutiny broke out. It ended in the handing over of India to the Government of the Crown. The effect of the conquest of India upon our foreign policy has been twofold. First, the direct necessity of taking certain strong places on the route to our great dependency, and our alliance with the Porte. From England to the East we hold a chain of posts which are essential to the safety of our communication, but which render us liable as time goes by to the maintenance constantly in the Mediterranean of a fleet at least equal to that of France and Italy combined. Secondly, our hold upon India has greatly increased our timidity in championing any great cause, and has turned our attention from the sea, where our real strength lies, to the land, on which our national aversion from conscription must always make us fight at a disadvantage. In India England is perforce a great military power; and this, which is wholly at variance with our traditions – for, as has been well said, we are a warlike, but not a military people – tinges the whole current of our foreign policy. Indian policy on more than one occasion has taken precedence of English; Asiatic ideas have had too great influence; we have, in short, what with fear of invasion, and dread of a rising in India itself consequent upon misfortune in Europe, lost all sense of proportion in considering the external relation of such a country as ours. Asiatic politics must inevitably enter largely into our calculations merely on the ground of our commercial interests;

but India, with its 60,000 European troops, is, as at present governed, a source of increasing weakness to the people of these islands, who may find themselves seriously hampered at a great national crisis by the necessity for protecting their countrymen in Hindustan. This will become more clear now that our frontier all but marches with that of a great and troublous military power. India, consequently, will prove a more disturbing element in our foreign policy of the future than it has been in the past.

With the Treaty of Paris, however, England may be said to have entered practically on the stage of permanent non-intervention in continental affairs. Our efforts to preserve peace when it was once understood that under no circumstances whatever would we go to war, became futile and even ludicrous. This was apparent with regard to the French campaign against Austria. Had we proclaimed our intention of siding with either party, war would not have been declared. But the establishment of the independence of Italy, by French arms first, and by Garibaldi's expedition afterwards, met with the cordial sympathy of the great mass of Englishman. Though the upper classes still clung to the Austrian alliance, the people were more clear-sighted, whilst Cavour's happy moderation reassured the middle class. Thus, all rejoiced at the rise of Italy into a great power, and the extraordinary reception accorded to Garibaldi by the democracy of London, gave evidence that the real feeling of Englishmen is with the peoples of the continent, and needs but a proper occasion to manifest itself in full force. The contest between the North and the South in America, brought this truth into stronger relief. Once more the upper and middle classes, as in 1848 and 1859, linked themselves with the side of reaction, and that side, unfortunately for their credit and influence, was this time the weaker. Nothing finer is recorded than the behaviour of the Lancashire operatives during that awful period of continuous want. The capitalists who employed them showed no such real perception of the truth, and their selfishness appeared in protesting against any scheme which might remove the hands, and thus perhaps raise wages on the return of trade. That by the way. The fact that the working class saw the issue lay between freedom and despotism, and clung to their opinion under every discouragement, is evidence of a capacity which needs but education and organization to have a deep effect in other fields of foreign policy.

The hare-brained French expedition to Mexico was the outcome of the American Civil War, and this eventually brought the French Empire to destruction. For no sooner was the shameless attack upon Denmark by Prussia and Austria at an end – when German influence again appeared in our counsels – than the two great Powers who took part in that act of brigandage fell out themselves. The cooler-headed brigand fell upon his neighbour, and by the victory of Sadowa the supremacy of Germany was gained by Prussia. Here, of course, was an end of all international law. Thenceforward we have been living in an epoch of wrong and robbery. France, crippled by the Mexican campaign, could not afford to help Austria against Prussia and Italy – merely, in fact, displaying her weakness to a watchful enemy. England counted for nothing in all this, and the only benefit which accrued to the peoples from the bloodshed and treachery was the annexation of Venice by Italy. The extension of the power of military Junker-ridden Prussia over the pacific old Bund could only be viewed with satisfaction by those who, whilst pretending to be Liberals, secretly sympathize with brute force so long as it is organized against the mass of mankind. In any case Prussia, still closely allied with Russia, became the first Power in Europe, and the next move was merely a matter of time and opportunity.

By the year 1870 England had not only ceased to have a continental policy, but she positively had not the least idea of what was going on. It is really alarming, especially at a time like the present, to note the depth of ignorance in the English

Foreign Office eleven years ago. At the very moment when the Frederick the Great of modern diplomatic Germany had made up his mind to strike France once for all, and had contrived to "localize" the war after his favourite fashion by arrangements with Russia and Italy, our Foreign Office had come to the conclusion that no elements of war, so much as remained in Western Europe at all. France was easily overthrown; and England, unfortunately for our credit and our interests, refused to help the Republic which rose upon the ruins of the Empire. Then, if the phrase ever meant anything, was the time to show the meaning of a real balance of power. France had been beaten; the Empire, with its wretched array of stock-jobbers and intriguers, had been swept away. So far we had no right to interfere; but the people of France were in nowise responsible for the errors of Napoleon; and a bold policy would have rallied Italy and Austria at once to our side, to prevent a brave nation from being crushed. That course was not adopted, and any remonstrance met with insolence from the German Government. Our position became indeed that for which our non-interventionists had striven. Of course further plots could be carried on independently of any consideration for the only Power in Europe which has no real interest except in fair play to the peoples.

It is needless to pass through the long and troubled period which began with the Austrian imperial intrigues in Bosnia and the Herzegovina, the Servian War, and can scarcely be said to have ended with the Treaty of Berlin. That a whole scheme was laid down for the partition of the Ottoman Empire by the renewed Holy Alliance, is clear. Russia, Germany, and Austria had each their portions assigned, whilst the advantages to be received by France and England were doubtless considered; perhaps the latter might be content with nothing at all. The Bulgarian atrocities helped Russia to carry out her part of the programme, though the weakness engendered by the war has certainly not been repaid by the advantages she has as yet

155

secured. England's part in the business has again been most unsatisfactory. A war in Europe was avoided; but a war in Asia was begun, which has saddled our impoverished dependency with a fearful expenditure. By showing, however, even a moderately bold front in Europe, the Conservative Government proved conclusively the influence which England could exert, if only casting aside all lust for territory, and all underhand intrigue, she stood once more with clean hands before the world as the resolute champion of justice and freedom, honesty and public faith. Then she could rally to her side the alliances of the future, beside which the possession of Cyprus, or even the control of Constantinople and Asia Minor would seem mean and contemptible. But the result of the game of brag which the last Government played was not creditable. Instead of holding forth a plain, intelligible policy to Englishmen, and appealing to them to stand by even a downright Tory self-assertion, there was a mixture of trimming and secrecy, of compromise and timidity, which spoke of divided counsels and irresolute minds. The people of England therefore refused to go "blind" into a business which combined secret agreements abroad with the threat of reaction in Ireland and at home. These, happily, are the days of democracy, publicity, and open speech. The statesman who is ambitious to lead England in such times must take the people into his confidence, and convince them that he is using their influence and their power not merely for selfish national interests, but for the best interests of Europe and the world.

That the result of our secret diplomacy and party foreign policy has not yet been fully seen is plain enough. Non-intervention to start with, and secret bargaining to end with, have landed us in a very unenviable position. The nation refused to countersign the policy of the Conservative Government, and the Liberals came in with the promise of a special understanding with France and perfect openness to the country. France has so far dissembled her love for the Liberal administration that she has kicked our Foreign Secretary downstairs at three bounds. Greece, the Commercial Treaty, and Tunis, are evidences of the perfect *entente cordiale* which exists. The last *coup* is the worst of all, for it came after assurances of the most solemn nature that nothing whatever was meant. Can we be surprised? A policy of pure selfishness has ended in our complete isolation. The behaviour of France is shameful, and contrary to her best interest. Granted. The treatment which we have received in the matter would in different times have led to a rupture of friendly relations between the two countries. But at this moment we cannot rely upon a single ally on the continent; and for all we know, arrangements may be contemplated which would occasion us very grave uneasiness.

For those who talk of non-intervention forget that we have entered into definite guarantees, which the least bellicose among us could not wish to shirk. The overthrow of international law, which is pretty complete now, would be fully accomplished indeed, if England were to withdraw from her defence of liberal little Belgium. We have had of late very valuable experience as to what the concert of Europe amounts to when booty is in the wind. It is more than probable that the redistribution of territory and power, which began in 1866, will not be confined to Eastern Europe. Should we desire, then, to see the same sort of morality, which is good enough for Turks, applied to Dutch, Belgians, and Swiss? The idea that justice influences either republics or empires in these days had better be laid aside for the present as the figment that it is. A power which could act as France has acted about Tunis, would have small scruple in using similar tactics nearer home.

But even more important to us than any bargaining which may be going on, is the general aspect of European affairs. We see four, not to say five, great Powers absolutely bowed down with the weight of their military expenditure; whilst the great country which in 1848 acted as the guardian of autocracy in Europe, hovers between bankruptcy and revolution. Whatever else may be doubtful, this is past all question, neither Germany nor Austria can permanently bear the strain of the tremendous armaments now kept up. For these armaments not only exhaust the resources of the several countries, but prepare the ground for internal revolution of the most serious character. It is not Russia alone which is honeycombed with secret societies and festering disaffection. There, indeed, the situation is graver than elsewhere. Over-taxation, the drain of produce to Western Europe, the influence of capitalism, and the break up of the Mir coming at a time of serious famine, have produced a state of affairs throughout the Empire which would probably lead to revolution in one shape or another, if the Nihilists had never been heard of. That extraordinary conspiracy is but the natural outcome of a still more remarkable condition below. Western civilization, with all its paraphernalia of stockjobbing, corruption, and extravagance, has been imposed on a country but just emerging from barbarism. Almost anything may occur in such circumstances. The murder of the late Czar shocked Europe: but the cruelties which led up to that crime were really even more shocking than the revenge. More people were swept off to Siberia without trial by the benevolent Alexander II than ever found their way thither within an equal period during the worst days of the reign of Nicholas. Now there is another Czar, who lives in constant fear for his life; and the recent changes seem to betoken a continuance of autocratic rule at home, combined possibly with a renewal of aggression abroad. Men live as in expectation of an earthquake; and the attacks upon the Jews and other money-lenders in Southern Russia look like the premonitory shocks.

If the disturbances do begin in earnest in Russia, they are almost certain to lap over into other countries. Already the grave social issues involved in the existing capitalist system as applied to agriculture and business are being debated with increasing earnestness all over Europe. In Germany the party of the Social Democrats has gained strength of late years to a surprising extent, notwithstanding the pressure of similar laws to those which we are now applying with such great success in Ireland. Conscription does but give the disaffected more confidence; and as they see that peaceful agitation is considered a crime, the propaganda might easily assume a more dangerous shape. A military system like that of Germany carries with it the certainty of its own destruction at no distant date. All Prince Bismarck's unscrupulous energy will not suffice to stop the current of ideas which show men how and why they are robbed and oppressed. In Austria the agrarian difficulty is assuming daily a graver aspect. Nor is it the less serious because the people have not as yet dissociated the agitation from religion or loyalty. They scarcely understand themselves how it is that capitalism and difference of value impoverish them. In France a party holding similar views to that of the Labour party in Germany, has been formed, and they alone have had the courage to protest against the attack on Tunis, as contrary to the interest and the true sense of morality of the French people.

How far these various socialist bodies in Russia, Germany, Austria, France, and Italy, would act together in any general programme may be doubtful. But these organizations -consisting almost exclusively of working men – alone seem to have grasped the truth that the people of the various countries have nothing to expect from war but loss and suffering; consequently they alone are prepared to consider existing difficulties with a view to their peaceful settlement. Men who hold that their class is undergoing suffering and misery because the workers of all nations are not sufficiently at one, will not be likely to foment those national hatreds which are generally turned to the aggrandisement of individuals. But this rising feeling of democracy, this growing disinclination of the men who work to be handled any longer for the advantage of emperors, aristocrats or even bond-buyers, is viewed with very uneasy eyes by the military powers of Europe. It is not the assassination of the late Czar, or threats against the present, which are drawing together "saviours of society" on the continent. They see that, let affairs in Russia take what turn they may, another and more serious '48 movement is going on below the surface, which they wish beforehand to encounter and defeat. Hence the attempts to bring about some understanding with reference to the surrender of political refugees, and the demands which have been made, or will be made, upon us.

Now arises an important question for us Englishmen – and especially for those of the working classes – to decide. Will they in the coming struggle between militarism and democracy lend their aid in any way to the former, or even stand aloof and see the peoples of Europe repressed as they were a generation since? I judge not. Jealousy of this or that nation there may be for a time, and French vanity and unfortunate spread-eagleism may render all combinations in Western Europe impossible. But with the rising feeling of democracy here at home, any understanding with reaction as in old days would be ruinous to the party which attempted it, as any effort to convert us into a military power may be fatal to our existing system of government. As time has passed on, it has become more and more clear that in the direction of the national inclination of the great majority of Englishmen lies at the same time the most advantageous policy for England. Lying apart from the continent of Europe, and practically free from the risk of invasion, we can not only shelter men who are driven from their country for mere political offences, but we can rightfully stand forth at the critical moment on behalf of those who at present think that England must necessarily range herself on the side of a conservatism which has come to be revolutionary. Each nation, doubtless, must work out its own social troubles; but a combination of despotisms can only be met and overcome by a combination of peoples. The true alliances for England in the future are the democracies of Europe, and her real strength is on the sea.

Notes

1. We have ordinarily less than three weeks' supply of food at hand. A naval combination which could blockade our ports for a fortnight, could starve us out. Two powers, acting together could even now have a stronger fleet in the Channel than we could command.

Conclusion

Thus in every direction the policy of the democracy is clear and well-defined. Freedom, social reorganization, thorough unity at home, justice, self-government, and consideration for our colonies and dependencies, and a warm friendship and ready assistance for the oppressed peoples abroad, – such is the work we are called upon to begin and carry out. Democracy, which the so-called "governing classes" jeer at as anarchy, incapacity, and self-seeking, means a close federation, first, of our own people, and next, of the workers of the civilized world. This is a policy not of to-day or of to-morrow, now to be taken up and again to be laid aside; it is an undertaking in which each can continuously bear his share, and hand on the certainty of success to his fellow.

The current of events will help on the cause of the people. Within the past generation greater changes have been wrought than in centuries of human existence before. For the first time in the history of mankind the whole earth is at our feet. Railways, telegraphs, steam communications, have but just begun to exercise an influence. Education and intercourse are breaking down the barriers of ages. The men who do the work of the world are learning from one another how it is that the poor and the miserable, the unfortunate and the weak, suffer and fall by the wayside. In our own country, which has led the way to the new stage of social development, all can see that the lot of the many is sad, whilst the few are rich and luxurious far beyond what is beneficial even to them. Our action in redress of these inequalities and better ordering of our affairs will guide and encourage the world. We, perhaps, alone among the peoples can carry out with peace, order, and contentment those changes which continental revolutionists have sought through anarchy and bloodshed. Religion, which should have helped in this striving for a happier period, has suffered the rich and powerful to twist its teachings to their own account. Now, therefore, is the time, in the face of difficulties and dangers which threaten from many quarters, for Englishmen of all classes, creeds, and conditions to push aside the petty bickerings of faction or the degrading influence of mere selfish interests, to the end that by sympathy and fellow-feeling for their own and for others they may hold up a nobler ideal to mankind. Such an ideal is not unreal or impracticable. Not as yet of course can we hope to realize more than a portion of that for which we strive. But if only we are true to one another, and stand together in the fight, the brightness of the future is ours – the day before us and the night behind. So, when those who come after look back to these islands as we now look back to Athens or Palestine, they shall say, – "This was glory – this true domination; these men builded on eternal foundations their might, majesty, dominion, and power."